NEW AGE
HEALING

QUEST FOR THE UNKNOWN

NEW AGE
HEALING

THE READER'S DIGEST ASSOCIATION, INC.

Pleasantville, New York/Montreal

Quest for the Unknown
Created, edited, and designed by DK Direct Limited

A Dorling Kindersley Book

DK Direct Limited

Series Editor Richard Williams
Senior Editor Sue Leonard
Editors Ellen Dupont, Maxine Lewis
Editorial Research Julie Whitaker

Senior Art Editor Susie Breen
Art Editor Mark Osborne
Designer Sara Hill
Picture Research Frances Vargo; **Picture Assistant** Sharon Southren

Editorial Director Jonathan Reed; **Design Director** Ed Day
Production Manager Ian Paton

Volume Consultants Arnold Desser, Reg Grant, Justin O'Brien
Contributors Caroline Boddie, John Harford, Robert Leichtman, Ann Lloyd,
Jane Lyle, Timothy Marris, John Andrew Miller, Susan Pinkus, Marilyn Rossner,
Frank Smyth, Christina Thomas, Geoffrey Wadlow, Ruth West

Illustrators Roy Flooks, Mike Shepherd, Matthew Richardson
Photographers Andrew Atkinson, Simon Farnhell, Andrew Griffin,
Mark Hamilton, Susanna Price, Alex Wilson

Library of Congress Cataloging in Publication Data

New Age healing
      p.   cm. — (Quest for the unknown)
  "A Dorling Kindersley book" — T.p. verso.
  Includes index.
  ISBN 0-89577-463-1
  1. Alternative medicine. 2. Holistic medicine. 3. New Age
movement. I. Reader's Digest Association. II. Series.
R733.N479 1992
615.5—dc20   92-16462

Printed in the United States of America

FOREWORD

*D*URING THIS CENTURY ORTHODOX Western medicine has made many
impressive advances in the diagnosis and treatment of disease:
X-rays, antibiotics, organ transplants, and ultrasound, to name
but a few. Yet this form of medicine, heavily reliant on powerful drugs,
intrusive investigative techniques, and surgery, has had a number of charges
leveled at it. One is that it treats symptoms without reference to the whole
person. Another is that it may create fresh illnesses in the patient. And yet
another is that it is imposed from without by clinicians with whom patients
may feel that they have no rapport, and for whom they may be just units on
a medical conveyor belt.

It is for these reasons that an increasing number of people are exploring
alternative therapies. Acupuncture, aromatherapy, autosuggestion, Ayurveda,
Bach flower remedies, bioenergetics, color therapy, faith healing, herbalism,
homeopathy, hypnosis, meditation, naturopathy, polarity therapy, rebirthing,
reflexology, tai chi, transactional analysis, yoga — all these, and many others,
are described in this volume, together with a number of unusual diagnostic
techniques. While such therapies may not suffer from the same drawbacks
as conventional medicine, the claims made for many of them are open to
question. We do not recommend using any alternative therapy in place of
orthodox medical practices. Increasingly, however, doctors are coming to
view some of these therapies as effective complementary treatments, to be
used in conjunction with conventional medicine. Throughout this volume,
we have tried to present a balanced view, taking into account the pros and
cons of each technique.

What many cases in this book demonstrate is the remarkable self-healing
power of the human mind, body, and spirit. Conventional medicine is
increasingly recognizing the value of this idea and may yet undergo a
revolution as it borrows more and more techniques from the alternative
movement. The medical maxim of the 21st century may well be
"heal thyself."

— *The Editors*

CONTENTS

FOREWORD
5

INTRODUCTION
RELEASE FROM DARKNESS
8

CHAPTER ONE
THE HEALING PRINCIPLE
18

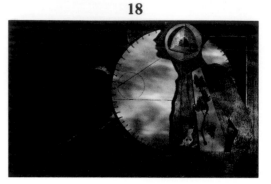

PERSONALITY AND PROGNOSIS
WISDOM FOR THE WORLD
KILL OR CURE
QUACKS
WISE WOMEN AND WITCHES
SHAMANISM
AMULETS AND TALISMANS
LIKE BY LIKE
CURING THE FAMOUS

CHAPTER TWO
THE POWER OF BELIEF
44

EXERCISING CONTROL
A HIGHER POWER
HEALING FROM AFAR
TUNING INTO THE DIVINE MIND
PAINLESS ECSTASY
CASEBOOK
THE GUIDING SPIRIT
PSYCHIC SURGERY

CHAPTER THREE
THE WISDOM OF THE EAST
66

A BALANCED DIET
THE MYSTERY OF THE PAINLESS NEEDLES
MEDITATION IN MOTION
DEMANDING JOURNEY
ELEMENTAL HEALING
HEALING PRESSURE
WHEELS OF ENERGY

CHAPTER FOUR
HEALTHY INFLUENCES
82

THE INFLUENCE OF THE STARS
CRYSTALS: LEGACY OF ATLANTIS?
THE HEALING STONES
IN SEARCH OF SERENITY
SHORTCUTS TO NIRVANA?
AUTOSUGGESTION
GOOD VIBRATIONS
AURA OF HEALTH
KIRLIAN PHOTOGRAPHY

CHAPTER FIVE
BODY WORK
106

STAGECRAFT
FREEING THE LIFE FORCE
THE MAGIC TOUCH
A HEAD START ON HEALTH
YOU ARE WHAT YOU EAT
ALLERGIC TO THE 20TH CENTURY
FIGHTING CANCER
HERBAL CURES
READING THE BODY
WINDOWS OF THE SOUL

CHAPTER SIX
HEALING THE PSYCHE
132

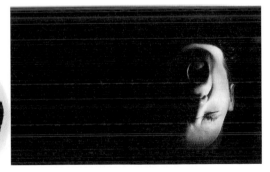

JOURNEYS TO HEALTH
CASEBOOKS

INDEX
142

RELEASE FROM DARKNESS

Those who claim to have been healed by the laying on of hands often say they feel a current of energy entering them. One June evening Tayja Wiger, a blind woman, experienced just such a force and from that moment her life was changed.

Tayja Wiger is a half-Sioux-Indian woman who was born in Minnesota in 1954. Her early life was one of suffering and fear. She was born partially blind and with cerebral palsy that restricted the use of her legs. She endured physical, emotional, and mental abuse and suffered epileptic seizures. Her sight deteriorated, and by the age of 17 she suffered from severe tunnel vision. She became a juvenile delinquent, a drug addict, an alcoholic, and, in 1980, was diagnosed as schizophrenic. Her sight grew progressively worse. In 1981 she was certified as legally blind.

That same year Wiger began attending classes provided by the Blind Awareness Project in Minnesota, whose aim was to try to get blind people to "see" by means of extrasensory perception (ESP). It was through her friends at the project that Wiger found herself, in June 1984, at the age of 30, attending a workshop on ESP and related subjects. This was held at Carleton College in Northfield, Minnesota, at the annual retreat of an inter-faith movement, the Spiritual Frontiers Fellowship.

The whole truth?

What follows is an account of the events that occurred at the healing service that concluded the retreat that night. These occurrences may appear to some to be the stuff of fantasy or the product of troubled or naive minds. In addition, Tajya Wiger's blindness, although medically verifiable, may have been psychosomatic. And the witnesses themselves may be judged by their presence in the congregation at a healing service to be more impressionable than most. Yet whatever reservations one may have about what happened to Tayja Wiger that evening, the incident was not an isolated one. Similar dramatic occurrences are reported every day in good faith by honest and reliable individuals.

> "It was an unusually hot evening....The rainbow hues beaming in through the stained-glass windows seemed to quiver in the warm air."

Sense of expectancy

The healing service, held in the college chapel, was attended by about 600 people, including Marilyn Rossner, Ph.D., a children's behavioral therapist and a doctor of special education. The extraordinary events of that day are described here by her.

❝ It was an unusually hot evening. In the chapel the swishing of the electric fans provided a constant accompaniment to the melodious tones of the organ. The rainbow hues beaming in through the stained-glass windows of the chapel seemed to quiver in the warm air.

₀ "Whether I imagined it or not I don't know, but there seemed to be a sense of expectancy among the congregation. A healer had delivered her quietly intoned meditation, 'The Keys to Spiritual Evolution and Healing,' and now the organ and choir sounded forth with unrestrained joy. It was as though this jubilant music were heralding what was soon to take place at the chapel.

"As well as being a trained scientist, I am also founder-president of the Spiritual Science Fellowship of Canada and an ordained minister of the International Council of Community Churches. And it was in this capacity that I was at the Retreat as a lecturer, together with my husband, John, who is a university professor as well as an Episcopalian minister.

"Facing the chapel altar were 30 empty chairs, in two rows. Behind each chair stood a healer, a member of the Retreat teaching staff. They included John and myself. Each member of the congregation was to sit briefly in one of these chairs, and a healer was to lay hands on him or her and ask for that person's healing in body, mind, and spirit.

Spirit control

"I relaxed and prayed, to ready myself for the healing of whoever would sit in the chair in front of me. It was at this point that I began to slip in and out of a light trance. I had become aware of the loving presence of my spirit control, the great Indian sage Swami Sivananda of Rishikesh. Sivananda had been a doctor, who had devoted most of his time to healing children and the poor and who had established clinics for the blind. Later he gave up medicine to become a

> **"Our breathing and heartbeat, our entire metabolism, seemed to become synchronized. I felt that my whole body and soul had become one with Tayja's."**

swami (Hindu religious instructor), concentrating on man's spiritual rather than physical ills. Today he is known as 'the Saint Francis of modern India.'

"Sivananda has been guiding me since I was a child. Now, from what he was saying to me, I knew that something extraordinary was about to happen. What it was I didn't know, but I had this inner certainty that it would take place.

The healing service

"By this time, as the music continued to pour forth exultantly, the ushers were guiding the congregation in an orderly procession from their pews to the empty chairs. Among those nearing us I noticed Tayja Wiger, a half-native-American woman to whom I had been briefly introduced the day before. Her eyes were almost closed and all that could be seen through the slits were two blank white segments like those unseeing eyes on the marble busts of antiquity.

"Tayja is a tall, physically imposing woman with strong features. On this memorable evening her rich, dark hair was braided, she wore a brightly patterned, red ceremonial Indian robe, and was barefoot. She moved haltingly, and an usher escorted her all the way to the vacant seats, since she had had to leave her Seeing Eye dog Daisy outside the chapel. Tayja was directed to the nearest empty seat, but for some reason she insisted on making her way along the row to the one in front of me.

"Soon all the chairs were occupied. I stretched out my arms and placed my hands on Tayja's head. Immediately I felt a current of energy course powerfully through me and I could feel myself beginning to vibrate all over. I covered Tayja's eyes with my hands. Suddenly our breathing and heartbeat, our entire metabolism, seemed to become synchronized. I felt that my whole body and soul had become one with Tayja's. Then I went into a trance, which apparently lasted about 10 minutes. I was conscious not only of the presence and power of Sivananda but of those of Christ and the Holy Spirit.

Miraculous event

"While in this trance I was conscious of very little of the miraculous event that took place during it. I only learned about it properly some time later, from the accounts of my husband and of friends who were present. Apparently, I began shaking Tayja's head so vigorously that it rolled about like a rag doll's. This was unusual for me — I usually carry out healing in a gentle way. As I shook Tayja, I was telling her intensely, over and over, 'You can see! You can see!'

"Tayja then stood up in front of me, and I am told that, gazing up at her, I exclaimed, 'Keep your eyes open. Let go of the past. It's all over, it's all over.'

"I can see!"

"Then Tayja cried out, in her deep, powerful voice, 'I can see! I can see the light! I can see you!' She looked around, laughing and crying at the same time.

"Tayja's expressions of joy brought the service to a halt. The organ stopped playing. When the congregation became aware of what had happened, they began applauding, gathering around Tayja, and letting their joy be known.

"Tayja asked to be taken outside the chapel, on to the lawn of the college campus, where she could see all the beauty of nature that she had been deprived of for so long in her world of darkness. One of the first things that Tayja asked to see was her dog, whom until then she had known only through touch and sound. When she set eyes on her, she was overjoyed to see at last this faithful dog, who from now on would be just a companion and no longer a guide.

> **"As Tayja looked at me I saw with wonderment that her eyes, which had been narrow and blank, were now the bright, wide eyes of a child. She had emerged from darkness into the light."**

"As Tayja looked at me I saw with wonderment that her eyes, which had been narrow and blank, were now the bright, wide eyes of a child. She had emerged from darkness into the light. **"**

Strange destiny

Cynthia Bend, one of the founders of the Blind Awareness Project, later co-authored with Wiger an account of the latter's life, *Birth of a Modern Shaman* (1987). In the book, Bend and Wiger report that soon after recovering her sight, Wiger had her eyes tested by the ophthalmologist who had declared her to be legally blind. The new report stated that Tayja's visual acuity was 20/20 in both eyes and that her field of vision was totally unrestricted — in short, that she had "regained her sight."

The authors also reveal that, while she was blind, Wiger believed that she was destined to be a shaman, an important figure in many cultures, including those of the American Indians. The shaman is a doctor-priest who is believed to possess the power of healing by using magic to mediate between this world and those beyond. After she regained her sight, Wiger did in fact act as a shaman and has conducted healing sessions. Many who have attended them claim to have been cured of a variety of disorders, some reportedly just as suddenly and completely as Wiger appears to have been cured of her blindness.

The work of the spirit guides

Wiger herself, after her cure, became for the first time physically and mentally well. She believes that the life force channeled through Marilyn Rossner was that of the spirit guides of many people present, including Wiger's own, all joined together to generate the healing energy that restored her sight.

Rossner herself says: "I believe that in the period before her sight was restored, Tayja was spiritually ready for this healing, so that it became a possibility. God, working through Christ, the Holy Spirit, Swami Sivananda, and my hands, turned that possibility into actuality."

COMMENT

We have selected the remarkable case of Tayja Wiger as our Introduction because it encapsulates several important aspects of modern alternative therapies. For example, it stresses the importance of a sick person using his or her own inner healing powers; it seemingly demonstrates that the power of belief may be able to bring about what appear to be cures that modern science can't readily explain; it recognizes, as previous ages did, that women may well have natural healing skills that men may lack; and it even suggests that the sudden release of pent-up psychic tension can provide dramatic relief from physical and mental ills.

Weighing the evidence

The case is also interesting because it raises questions of a type that we shall encounter in the rest of this volume. For example, is there any solid medical evidence that Wiger was physically rather than psychologically blind before her cure? Indeed, four years before she was certified as legally blind, a medical report suggested that Wiger's visual problems might be hysterical, and later she agreed with this diagnosis herself. Hysterical blindness can produce the same physical symptoms as organic blindness and is usually the result of severe stress. Is it possible that Marilyn Rossner's violent shaking of Wiger's head somehow jolted her out of what was simply a condition originally induced by mental stress?

There is also the evidence cited in *Birth of a Modern Shaman* that during her attendance at the Blind Awareness Project, Wiger could correctly identify colors and objects in pictures given to her. According to the authors, this was the result of ESP. Many people, while not questioning the good faith of the women making these claims, might question the accuracy of the explanation provided.

Then there is the testimony of those at the healing service that they saw an instantaneous transformation in the visible condition of Wiger's eyes. How reliable are these witnesses? The congregation present that day could not be described as a representative cross section of the community. Eighty percent of those present were members of the Spiritual Frontiers Fellowship, an organization committed in part to exploring the paranormal. It must be said that many of these people, in attending a service, would have been predisposed to believe in a miracle cure produced by the laying on of hands.

Belief and skepticism

Throughout this volume we shall see similar opposing arguments – belief and skepticism warring with each other and taking us first in one direction, then in another. But whatever the true nature of Tayja Wiger's blindness, whatever the true nature of the restoration of her sight, there is little doubt that something truly extraordinary took place in the chapel of Carleton College on that June evening in 1984. At the very least, Tayja Wiger experienced a transformation in the quality of her life as a result of the events of the evening that conventional medicine had not been able to provide, and cannot explain.

> The sudden release of pent-up psychic tension can provide dramatic relief from physical and mental ills.

CHAPTER ONE

The Healing Principle

In an age dominated by orthodox medicine's powerful drugs, high-tech equipment, and complex operations, more and more people are turning to one of the many forms of alternative therapy in their search for physical and spiritual well-being.

Though the count varies and definitions change, there now appear to be some 120 alternative therapies in existence, therapies that for the most part differ as radically from the practices of conventional medicine as they do from each other as they pursue their elusive goal: to link body and mind — and enhance inner healing.

Some of these techniques require long and intensive training, while others demand only minimal part-time instruction. Some therapies were developed relatively recently; others have been in use since

HIGH COST OF HEALING

A strong incentive for exploring complementary treatments is the increasing awareness that orthodox medicine can hurt as well as heal, often because it has far-reaching effects; drugs meant to kill malignant cells, for example, can also damage healthy ones. This iatrogenic (doctor-created) disease is now a serious problem, and practitioners of both conventional and alternative medicine fear that a percentage of hospital patients may be there because the treatment given to cure them has created new illness, which in turn needs medical treatment, and so on.

Modern drugs

The nature of modern pharmacology means that this is unlikely to change; today's drugs

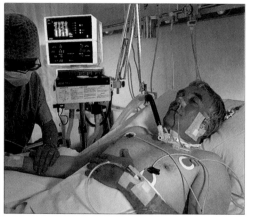

Machine-made medicine
Modern equipment monitors almost every change in the patient's condition, but it can be frightening and intrusive.

can be likened to powerful bullets designed to destroy killer diseases.

In addition, the cost of finding and producing modern cures has led to a constant increase in health costs. This might encourage those responsible for investigating alternative disciplines to recall the view of the 16th-century Swiss physician Paracelsus: "I seek not to enrich the apothecaries," he said, "but to cure the sick."

earliest times. These therapies are known as *alternative* because they are generally not taught as part of orthodox medical training; in fact, most doctors would urge that they be used with great caution. They should certainly never be used in place of or in preference to conventional medicine. (It must be stressed at this point that if you have any health problems, you should see your doctor immediately — orthodox medicine still offers the most effective treatment for most ailments.)

Some therapies, such as osteopathy for example, are more widely accepted in orthodox medical circles than others, however, and thus are sometimes used in addition to conventional medicine. Hence many practitioners prefer the term *complementary* to describe the role of such therapies as part of a multi-disciplinary approach to healing that includes conventional medicine. Other adherents prefer to emphasize the term *holistic*, which reflects clearly the importance of dealing with the whole person rather than a specific symptom or disease, and of evaluating his or her body and mind and way of life.

Complete healing systems

The most complex and sophisticated of the alternative therapies are the complete healing systems. They generally tend to include theories about the causes of illness as well as systems of diagnosis and treatment. Their practitioners have usually undergone many years of extensive formal training and may have set up regulatory bodies with strict professional guidelines.

One of the oldest of these systems is traditional Oriental medicine, which

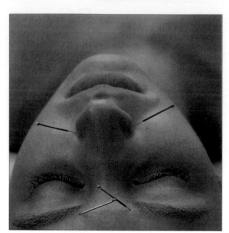

Points of view
In Chinese medicine, illness is thought to result from interruptions to the energy flow, or chi. Acupuncture needles are used to stimulate this flow.

includes acupuncture, acupressure, and a type of massage known as shiatsu (which is based on acupressure), along with many other complemetary techniques. Other examples include homeopathy, herbalism, and the musculo-skeletal discipline of chiropractic, which the British Medical Association has recently studied and declared to be considerably more effective than physiotherapy for the relief of back pain and related problems.

Gaining in popularity in the West during the last few years is the traditional Hindu healing system known as Ayurvedic medicine (from the Sanskrit words *ayur*, meaning life, and *veda*, meaning knowledge). This has a completely holistic structure, a heavy

Eastern remedies
This Indian apothecary displays her spices and herbs on a hot, crowded street in Hyderabad. Herbal remedies play an important role in Ayurvedic medicine, the traditional system of India.

◗ PAGE 22

PERSONALITY AND PROGNOSIS

Medical doctors are becoming increasingly aware of the powerful effect that both general temperament and a particular state of mind can have on a patient's susceptibility to a wide variety of illnesses, and also on his or her ability to recover from sickness.

THE TERM PSYCHOSOMATIC (from the Greek words *psyche*, meaning "mind or soul," and *soma*, meaning "body") is often used to refer to imaginary symptoms. Yet what it actually describes is illness that is caused by emotional disturbance, such as some cases of heart disease or stomach ulcers. This important concept has always been at the center of holistic traditions (for their adherents, *all* illness, in a sense, is psychosomatic), but orthodox medical research seems increasingly to be emphasizing the same approach. Doctors have long accepted the contribution of stress to such conditions as heart disease and high blood pressure, and have identified a link between personality type and cardiac health.

Stress and illness
During the late 1980's, a study by Dr. David Ragland and Dr. Richard Brand from the University of California, Berkeley, indicated that people who are chronically cynical, hostile, angry, suspicious, and mistrustful are twice as likely to have coronary artery blockages as those who have calmer, more trusting, and less judgmental personalities. And recent studies suggest that the development and progress of many different types of cancer may also be linked with the personality and emotional responses of the patient.

Health and happiness
In his 1989 book, *The Holistic Approach to Cancer*, British lecturer Dr. I. C. B. Pearce maintained that lonely, isolated people, or those who are unable to express negative feelings like anger, grief, despair, or pain, are more likely to develop some form of cancer.

Other studies indicate that cancer may appear significantly more often during the two years following severe emotional stress or loss of some kind (spouse,

Cancer may appear significantly more often during the two years following severe emotional stress or loss of some kind (spouse, job, home) than at other times.

job, or home, for example) than at other times. In terms of recovery, patients who have strong faith in either their medical care or their own powers of self-help and healing have a considerably better prognosis than those who feel completely powerless, and therefore accept decline and death as inevitable.

Similarly, many experts are beginning to suspect that emotional well-being is an important constituent of a healthy immune system. This theory may be borne out in some patients' personal experiences: they find, for example, that colds and other infections seem to take hold more frequently during periods of deep personal unhappiness and despair than at other, happier times.

The medical establishment may have been slow to accept the links between mind and body because orthodoxy finds it necessary to pin down and measure the causes and effects of disease, and therefore may be less comfortable with the complexity of human emotions.

Linking mind and body
In complete contrast, many alternative systems support the principle that mind and body should never be separated. As a result, their practitioners investigate the psychological state of all their patients, whatever symptoms they present. Even physically oriented therapists such as reflexologists tend to note the particular way in which each patient's body language indicates his or her state of mind; a rigid jaw and tight shoulders can indicate tension and stress, for example, whereas a slumped or round-shouldered posture may suggest feelings of depression.

In a surprisingly large number of cases, physicians practicing orthodox medicine have found that isolating and dealing with emotional problems can have a positive effect on illness or disability.

dependence on herbalism, and a strong emphasis on preventing, as well as curing, the particular illness.

Diagnostic techniques

Alternative medicine includes a wide range of diagnostic techniques. These include, for example, iridology, in which the eyes, particularly the irises, are believed to reveal signs of various different illnesses; kinesiology, which seeks to detect allergies by examining muscles and testing their resistance to pressure; and hair analysis, which claims to be able to detect dietary and some other deficiencies.

Perhaps the most unusual of these is aura diagnosis. Adherents of this peripheral therapy claim that the body's magnetic field is seen as an "aura," which is an area of glowing light around the body whose size, shape, color, and general characteristics practitioners believe can indicate the location of disease or other forms of weakness in the body.

Although some people claim to have benefited from these techniques, there is very little hard evidence to prove their effectiveness.

Complementary therapies

As the name implies, complementary therapies — such as reflexology (a complex form of foot massage), aromatherapy (a method of treating illness using highly scented essential oils), massage, spiritual healing (a holistic treatment that attempts to heal by promoting harmony of mind, body, and spirit), and hydrotherapy (water treatment) — exist alongside orthodox medicine, and in some cases, with its active support.

Self-help measures

Like complementary therapies, self-help measures are not intended to replace orthodox medical treatment. Instead they offer skills and techniques that people can learn and use in order to feel more relaxed, happier, and healthier.

> **Medical doctors have come to appreciate the value of some practices they once ridiculed.**

Among such systems are certain forms of relaxation therapy, including techniques such as meditation, yoga, and various types of breathing exercises, in addition to specially designed eating programs – such as vegetarian, vegan, low-protein, or high-fiber diets.

As time has passed, medical doctors have come to appreciate the value of practices they once ridiculed, such as chiropractic and even meditation. Similarly, ancient treatments long dismissed as old wives' tales are found to be based on sound medical principles. Certainly, the entire field of complementary medicine is now gaining new respect in conventional medical circles. Perhaps some of today's "alternative" therapies will be brought into the mainstream of orthodox medical practice in the not-too-distant future.

THE IMAGE OF THE WHOLE
Some commentators on alternative medicine, such as theoretical physicist Fritjof Capra, author of *The Tao of Physics* (1975), extend the theory of holism by borrowing from quantum physics the concept that each component of a larger entity may contain an image of the whole. Applied to alternative medicine, this could explain therapies like reflexology, where treatment applied to one small part of a person (an area on the foot in the case of reflexology) may affect the whole body.

Footsore
Practitioners of reflexology believe that illness shows up as a tender area on the foot, which is then treated by using specialized massage techniques.

Body of belief
The natural grace of animals inspired ancient yoga teachers to develop postures that benefit body, mind, and spirit.

WISDOM FOR THE WORLD

Rudolf Steiner believed that he could improve people's physical and spiritual health by helping them to relinquish their attachment to the material world. He believed that they would thereby regain the links they once had with their own inner spirit.

ORN IN AUSTRIA IN 1861, Rudolf Steiner was a pioneer advocate of the holistic approach and one of the first modern thinkers to investigate the apparent link between natural science and the world of the spirit.

The son of a railway official, Steiner studied mathematics, physics, and chemistry at the University of Vienna. Feeling strongly that conventional education and wisdom were restricted by their ties to the physical world, he set out to redress the balance in himself by developing

> He set out to redress the balance in himself by developing his "higher senses," perceptions that were independent of the five senses.

his "higher senses," perceptions that were independent of the five senses and that could therefore establish in him a "knowledge produced by the higher self in man."

The first strong influence on Steiner's thinking was the German philosopher and poet Johann Wolfgang von Goethe, whose scientific works he edited at the Goethe Archive in Weimar from 1889 until 1896. From Goethe, Steiner learned to look at science in a different way, and to search for a spiritual purpose in all forms of life.

The Christian spirit

Later, in 1902, Steiner became general secretary of the German branch of the mystical (and later discredited) Theosophical Society founded by Madame Helena Blavatsky, an experience that gave him a vocabulary with which to describe the world of the spirit. Theosophy, however, had its roots in Hinduism and also concerned itself with the occult, whereas Steiner's philosophy was strongly Christ-centered. As a result, he established, in 1912, the Anthroposophical Society, in Dornach, Switzerland. Anthroposophy (meaning

Rudolf Steiner
Pioneer advocate of the holistic approach.

"wisdom for the world") brought together the teachings of East and West in its holistic view of both man and the universe. A core belief of anthroposophy was that all things – art, science, philosophy, politics, drama, and architecture – are dynamically interrelated.

During the last seven years of his life, Steiner applied anthroposophy to medicine, and lectured physicians on the subject, suggesting that illness does not necessarily reflect a mechanical breakdown of the body, but rather a disturbance in the balance between man's four constituents. These were, in Steiner's view, physical body, etheric body (which houses the forces of growth), astral body (emotions and drives), and ego (consciousness of self). He also identified three body systems: the nerve-sense system, the rhythmic system, and the metabolic system.

Wisdom in practice

Anthroposophical medicine today has close links with homeopathy, and the School of Spiritual Science in Switzerland offers a postgraduate course in the subject for doctors. In continental Europe, there are more than a thousand anthroposophical doctors, and two general and eight specialist hospitals. In the United States and Britain, however, anthroposophy is used most widely in the care and teaching of mentally handicapped and emotionally disturbed children.

Spiritual home
The headquarters of the Anthroposophical Society in Dornach, Switzerland, was designed by Steiner and built in 1922 from molded concrete. Like the structure it replaced, which had been destroyed by fire, this building was called the Goetheanum, after Goethe, the man who inspired Steiner's early work.

KILL OR CURE

"I firmly believe that if the whole materia medica as now used could be sunk to the bottom of the sea, it would be all the better for mankind — and all the worse for the fishes."
Oliver Wendell Holmes

IN 1860, PHYSICIAN AND JURIST Oliver Wendell Holmes, then professor of anatomy at Harvard, made this comment on the contribution of medical drugs toward curing disease. Holmes put considerably more faith in judicious doses of wine and opium, either of which would have been more pleasant (and probably more effective) than many of the cures commonly prescribed, since most of these were based on the theory that all illness could be cured by dramatic purging or bleeding.

At the time, massive doses of toxic drugs such as antimony were prescribed to expel poisons through a technique known as purging. The only real alternative

---

Bloodletting, as late as the 19th century, was said to cure mania, headaches, epilepsy, and eye infections.

---

preparations were the widely touted but mostly useless patent medicines, which had value principally for those who made, advertised, and sold them.

The other stock treatment was bloodletting, and it was a long time before doctors realized that this was at best useless, and at worst fatal. A practice dating back to ancient Greece, bloodletting was used for various complaints, and as late as the 19th century was said to cure mania, headaches, epilepsy, and eye infections. Bloodletting was accomplished in one of four ways. Arteriotomy

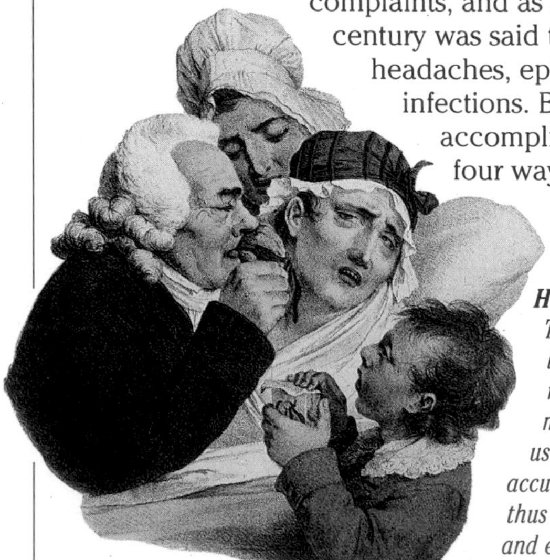

Healing wound
The discredited leech has been rediscovered by modern surgeons, who use it to suck away accumulations of blood, thus aiding circulation and encouraging the healing of skin grafts.

Patent poetry
This 1891 advertising poster makes the extravagant claim that "to compare other female tonics with this is to compare a lighted candle with the sun."

Rough remedy
In this early-19th-century print, entitled A Gentle Emetic, a well-meaning physician tries to cure his patient by making him vomit.

Soothing waters
Faith in the healing properties of water exists throughout the world. Believers claim that bathing in mineral-rich waters, for example, can cure a variety of illnesses and diseases.

Flow chart
This 1928 reproduction of a 1552 woodcut illustrates the various points on the body where bloodletting can be performed.

Relieving the pressure
In many cultures bleeding was believed to release "bad blood" and pressure caused by disease.

or venesection (opening an artery or vein directly) was very common, as was scarification (making scratches or small cuts), with and without cupping (which involved quickly placing a flame in a cup or glass, removing it, then applying the glass to the body; the partial vacuum created inside the cup made it attach itself to the flesh by suction, thereby increasing the flow of blood). The final method — and one of the most popular — was leeching. Dozens of leeches might be attached to a patient to suck out "evil vapors" along with the blood.

In the 17th century the eminent scientists and physicians William Harvey (who first discovered how the heart and circulatory system work) and Thomas Sydenham (considered the founder of clinical medicine) both believed in bleeding. Over a century later, it seems likely that George Washington's death might have been caused by this dangerous practice. His doctor, Benjamin Rush, bled him four times in order to treat a cold. The following day the president died.

Bleeding to death
Numerous fatalities were probably caused in such a way, yet opposition to the technique was generally mild and ineffectual. One of the earliest dissenters was Dr. Louis of the Charité Hospital in Paris in the early 19th century. While trying to assess the best day for bleeding pneumonia patients, he discovered that the longer treatment was delayed, the better the outcome for the patient. The degree to which this flew in the face of accepted wisdom is illustrated by Dr. Louis's apologetic comment that "it is only with hesitation that I have decided to publish [my findings]." By contrast, hydrotherapy (the use of water to treat

Essential fluid
Based on the belief that water is the essence of life, hydrotherapy has long been used to treat a wide variety of complaints.

illness) was regularly attacked and ridiculed by doctors. Yet it was not only harmless — in some cases it might have been extremely effective. The capacity of water to soothe aches and wounds has been acknowledged since ancient times. The Greeks and Romans believed strongly in mineral or hot spring bathing, and the sick were often given these waters to drink. Both customs were revived in 14th-century England, and spas soon became common throughout Europe. By the 19th century the Bohemian healer Vincenz Preissnitz and the Bavarian priest Sebastian Kneipp had made "taking the waters" in one form or another a highly fashionable practice for a wide variety of different ailments, real or imagined.

Soothing waters
Unlike purging and bleeding, hydrotherapy often produced real benefits, probably due to one of its basic principles, that of "action and reaction." When heat is applied to the skin it draws blood to the surface, while cold drives it deeper into the tissues. Standard hydrotherapy baths — hot, cold, and alternate hot and cold — make use of these effects to increase the blood's circulation and create temperature conditions related to the ailment in question.

A standard treatment of equally long standing, but of almost no use (and with greater potential for causing harm) was gynecological surgery. Hysteria (the word comes from the Greek for "womb") was from earliest times labeled a woman's condition. It was believed to be weakness of mind caused by a diseased womb and resulting in loss of bodily control. The apparently simple cure — surgically

> **Dozens of leeches might be attached to a patient to suck out "evil vapors" along with the blood.**

removing the womb — was practiced well into the Victorian era.

Many female nervous disorders were thought to originate in the reproductive system. Surgical removal of the ovaries was the standard cure for disorders such as epilepsy, as well as for mental illness. Even as late as the 20th century, hysterectomies were performed as a treatment for non-specific backache.

Indeed, a surprisingly large number of other irrational and ill-conceived treatments have been used during the enlightened 20th century: for example, total tooth extraction for either rheumatoid arthritis or cancer, vasectomy for rejuvenation, and blood dialysis for the treatment of patients suffering from schizophrenia. Even in 1978, a report entitled *Assessing the Safety and Efficacy of Medical Technology* (published by the Office of Technology Assessment, an arm of the U.S. Congress) stated that "only 10 to 20 percent of all procedures currently used in medical practice have been shown to be efficacious by controlled trial." This is despite the considerable resources invested in testing conventional treatments. Michael Rawlins, Professor of Clinical Pharmacology at the University of Newcastle upon Tyne in England believes strongly that a system of enforced double-blind controlled trials, plus special training in risk-benefit assessment, is the only solution. We have, Rawlins warns, seen only the introduction of truly rational therapeutics, "not yet its blossoming."

The capacity of water to soothe aches and wounds has been acknowledged since ancient times.

Magnetic corset

Electrical energy
In the mid-19th century some doctors believed that many diseases and chronic conditions were caused by electrical disturbances. Taking advantage of this theory, the London Medical Battery Company advertised a range of appliances designed to cure everything from writer's cramp to epilepsy.

Electropathic belt

THE FOUR HUMORS

The ancient concept of the four humors occupies an important place in the development of Western medicine, since it represents the first attempt to dissociate theories about illness and disease from the realm of gods and their whims. Instead, it emphasized rational causes based on both observation and examination.

First identified by the Greek physician Hippocrates, these humors (named after the Latin word meaning "moisture"), corresponded to the four fluids believed to govern the body: blood (from the heart), yellow bile (from the liver), black bile (from the spleen), and phlegm (from the brain). Disease was thought to occur when the balance of these humors was disturbed, either by external factors such as climate, occupation, and diet, or by inherent temperament and physical constitution.

Although Hippocrates had much to say about the causes of disease, he had little to offer by way of cure, preferring to rely on the "healing power of nature." This approach did not really change until the second century A.D., when the Roman physician Galen was influential. He believed that humoral excess or deficiency could be adjusted with drugs. To put his theories into practice, he produced extraordinary mixtures of traditional herbal remedies and new mineral and animal concoctions, such as dried camel dung and powdered rhinoceros horn. Some of his prescriptions required a hundred or more different substances.

Temperamental types
Later, in the Middle Ages, the association between humor and temperament was established. Thus a person with an excess of yellow bile was held to be "choleric" — quick to anger, jaundiced, ambitious, revengeful, and shrewd. And too much blood was said to result in a "sanguine" nature (from the Latin word *sanguis*, meaning "blood"), one that was optimistic, enthusiastic, and excitable. Similarly, black bile was considered responsible for a "melancholy" temperament, and phlegm for a stolid, impassive, "phlegmatic" one.

Some of these ideas remained in medical currency as late as the 1850's. Although they have now been discounted, traces remain in our language, for instance when we say that someone is in a "good" or "bad" humor.

Temperamental fluids
The title page of Septem Planetae (The Seven Planets), a 16th-century work by Gerard de Jode, is illustrated with personifications of the four humors.

QUACKS

When illness and disability strike, they leave people especially vulnerable. From the earliest times, there has never been a shortage of self-styled doctors who are unprincipled enough to take advantage of this weakness.

Healing harmonies
The tonic-peddling quack, impersonated on the English music hall (vaudeville) stage, is commemorated on the cover of an early-20th-century song sheet.

ROM THE 16TH CENTURY onward, doctors and apothecaries began to be recognized as scientists, to have their training and practice regulated to some degree, and to charge appropriate fees for their services. As a result, there quickly emerged a parallel body of charlatans, or quacks, who offered miraculous cures to those too poor, too ignorant, or too frightened to consult a doctor or druggist. These spurious practitioners continued to thrive for several hundred years, mainly because for most of that time, orthodox medicine had very little to offer that was better than the pills, potions, contraptions, and outlandish techniques of the quacks.

False hopes
Today, when most people know about, and have access to, advanced healing techniques, the health market supports fewer and fewer charlatans. Yet there remains an unscrupulous core of quacks who continue to offer false hopes to desperate people; in particular those suffering from arthritis, cancer, and mental illness, and also those seeking to slow the effects of aging. In 1984 the U.S. House of Representatives Select Committee on Aging recognized this problem by defining a quack as "anyone who promotes medical remedies known to be false...for a profit." The committee estimated that quackery costs the American public $10 billion per year.

Fair game
Country fairs gave quack doctors the ideal opportunity to dazzle the crowds with their theatrical pitches and extravagantly false claims. This typical fairground scenario is illustrated with a pen-and-ink wash by Thomas Rowlandson (1756–1827).

Feet of clay
This decorative Meissen pottery grouping consists of a grandly attired quack doctor with his pet monkey and his "zany" or traditional masked clown.

Eye opener
William Read, an illiterate Scottish tailor, set himself up as an oculist in the early 1700's and was later knighted by Queen Anne for his services to her.

African scene
Outside his Lusaka practice, a Zambian quack displays this list of his specialities, which range from preventing snakebites to strengthening marriages and curing tuberculosis.

Fatal fellows
William Hogarth's 1736 engraving "The Company of Undertakers" includes three contemporary quacks. In the middle of the top row is one of the most infamous, Bonesetter Crazy Sally Mapp, who despite her name, was credited with considerable orthopedic knowledge and skill.

Purveyor of potions
In the 17th century the term "mountebank" was used to describe someone who sold quack medicines from a platform. One of the best-known was the Dutchman Hans Buling, who hawked his wares in London at Covent Garden. This 1670 engraving of Buling with his box of potions is after a painting by M. Laroon.

Unnecessary solutions
A colorful cartoon dated 1814 satirizes both rampant hypochondria and the proliferation of unqualified apothecaries.

WISE WOMEN AND WITCHES

Many prominent figures in the world of New Age healing are women. This reflects an ancient tradition of women taking responsibility for nurturing and healing.

WATER WAYS

In early civilizations, one of the few superstitions to survive the increasing male domination of religion was the connection of wells or springs with curative powers. Water, one of life's basic necessities, was still associated with earth-mother goddesses and femininity; so female deities and spirits invariably guarded these sources of cleansing, renewal, and healing. Many wells and springs, originally named for pagan goddesses, were later rechristened after female saints. The link between healing women and water is also illustrated by the frequent appearance of wells tended by witches or old women in legend and folklore.

A visionary site
Joan of Arc's well near Bois-Chenu, Domrémy-la-Pucelle, France, marks the spot where she had her first vision. Guarded by her statue, the well still gives water which is said by some to have remarkable healing powers.

LINKED BY THEIR BIOLOGY WITH FERTILITY, and thus with the whole pantheon of nature, women portrayed as earth-based mother goddesses were worshiped throughout the ancient world. The power to heal was associated with these goddesses who could also create life. Thus the possession of healing skills was a natural extension of women's nurturing roles as mothers and givers of life.

In addition, early civilizations depended on women to gather leaves, fruits, and nuts for food. Later, when men began to hunt, women's association with plants continued to evolve, and they learned not only how to grow crops, but also how to use them in a wide variety of ways. This primitive blending of divinity, nurturing, and knowledge of the medicinal properties of herbs formed the basis, at least in part, for a tradition of female healing that held sway for centuries.

Medicine and religion

Throughout early history, medicine and religion were intertwined. In ancient Sumer, Assyria, Greece, and Egypt, the priestesses were in charge of curing the sick.

> ## The possession of healing skills was a natural extension of women's nurturing roles as mothers and givers of life.

In Egypt, queens were often successful healers too; Cleopatra, for example, was a noted physician.

As the nature of society changed, however, from the female-centered activities of gathering and nurturing to more male-oriented farming and trading, the masculine role became increasingly important. And this was reflected in the development and dominance of male sky gods, such as the Egyptian Ra and the Greek Zeus. As a result, women's role as healers was eroded and gradually diminished, and medicine began to develop solely as a male prerogative.

In ancient Greek legend, for example, Asclepius was the god of medicine and Hygeia was the goddess of health. But as the centuries passed, the goddess, once

Asclepius's equal, became known first as one of his daughters along with her sister Panacea, and later as his wife. But although no longer as powerful, Hygeia remained the guardian of health, and people still worshiped her, appealing to her to bless them with the gift of health. Today the sisters' names have contributed two common words to our language: hygiene (which means practices conducive to health) and panacea (remedy for all ills).

Helen of Troy, although celebrated for her great beauty, was also a noted healer, and Homer refers to her knowledge of drugs in his epic poem the *Odyssey*. The philosopher Aristotle, who was also a pioneering biologist whose work contributed much to medicine, was actively assisted by his wife Pythias, who played a significant part in his research.

In ancient Rome, the scholar Pliny the Elder asserted that female healers should be so humble that after they were dead, no one would know that they had ever lived. Despite these extreme views, however, medical knowledge often formed part of an aristocratic woman's education. Octavia, for example, wife of Mark Antony, wrote a book of remedies. This included a potion to relieve a sore throat that consisted of natural ingredients such as honey, myrrh, anise,

and caraway — a mixture very similar to those prepared by our grandmothers over 2,000 years later.

The Roman way of birth

The skills involved in assisting childbirth, however, were valued in Rome, and midwives were honored after each safe delivery. There were three kinds of midwives: the *obstetrix*, who delivered the baby; the *nutrix*, who helped the new mother to breast-feed; and the *ceraria*, a priestess of the mother goddess, Ceres, who was responsible for the child's care.

It was in Rome, too, during the second century A.D., that a female healer-physician named Aspasia achieved some degree of acclaim, and

> ## Before the Renaissance, women still had an important healing role within their families and communities.

indeed, her instructions for preventing miscarriage — avoid worrying, violent exercise, and chariot riding — were down-to-earth, practical, and generally effective.

During the years after the fall of Rome and before the Renaissance, women still had an important healing role in their families and communities. This period was known as the Dark Ages because the knowledge and learning of the ancient Greeks and Romans had been lost. It was a time when women's healing skills remained important, since there were few trained physicians.

Female physicians and midwives

Women were not usually licensed to practice medicine; in England, they were forbidden to, while in other European countries, they were few in number. One of these rare female physicians was Trotula, a talented doctor who taught during the 11th century at the medical

TRIAL BY PREJUDICE

In the late Middle Ages, one woman who practiced medicine in defiance of the establishment was Jacoba Felicie. Arrested in Paris in 1322, she argued her case with great eloquence: "It is better and more seemly that a wise woman learned in the art should visit a sick woman and inquire into the secrets of her nature and her hidden parts, than that a man should do so, for whom it is not lawful to see and seek out the aforesaid parts."

Good references

Felicie's patients testified to her skills, but the court ruled against her: Although she was allowed a limited practice, she was forbidden to receive payment. Nevertheless, the court records contain a telling tribute: "She was wiser in the art of surgery and medicine than the greatest master or doctor in Paris."

A second opinion

This 1651 engraving illustrates society's disapproval of female healers by depicting an angel replacing an old woman with a male physician at the bedside of a sick man.

Healing trio
These marble figures from ancient Rome represent Hygeia and Asclepius flanking Telesphoros, a demon member of the latter's medical retinue.

Female specialist
The medieval healer Trotula as shown in a 14th-century manuscript.

SHAMANISM

Shamanistic systems of magic are so ancient that they may even date back to the Stone Age. In a wide range of different cultures, shamans are believed to have access to the kingdom of the spirits, and therefore may influence the causes of disease and death.

A COMBINATION OF PHYSICIAN, magician, witch, and untutored psychotherapist, the shaman is essentially a medicine man or, occasionally, woman. The word is thought to come from the Russian/Tungus language of Siberia. Yet basic shamanistic rituals, although they have numerous cultural variations, are remarkably consistent wherever they may be found — from the Indians of North America to the Lapps of northern Scandinavia.

High priests

Fundamentally, shamans are believed to mediate between our world and those forces beyond it. Their functions include foretelling the future, controlling a wide variety of different events and circumstances (including the weather), seeking food sources, healing the physically and mentally ill, and acting as a cohesive central figure for their own groups or tribes.

In different cultures around the world, the term shaman covers healers, prophets, rainmakers, witch doctors, mediums, herbalists, and storytellers. Such figures are usually "called" to their vocation through powerful dreams, strange visions, or traumatic crises.

Shamanistic initiation is generally accompanied by ritualistic death and rebirth ceremonies, often entailing fasting or physical wounding. By abandoning elements of ordinary life, the shaman claims that he can contact the spirits, with whom he must work in the future.

Ritual use of toxic and narcotic plants to induce an altered state of consciousness is a typical shamanistic practice. Siberian shamans, for example, drink an infusion of a tiny amount of the poisonous mushroom *Amanita muscaria*, while certain American Indian shamans use the hallucinatory peyote cactus.

A wide knowledge of plant lore is another of the shaman's traditional strengths. Ethnobotany, the science of seeking native botanic cures, is now a growing field of study, and has attracted much attention from scientists and even from major drug companies.

Soul catcher
This device was used by shamans of the Tlingit Indian tribe of the Northwest coast to prevent the soul from leaving the body. They believed that if an evil force tempted the soul out of the body, its owner would fall ill or die.

Natural selection

Perhaps the most dominant characteristic of shamanism is its almost magical harmony with the natural world. Indeed, its origins probably lie in observations of animals and birds made by our ancestors. It was probably from watching wild creatures that early humans gained knowledge of what plants were poisonous, where water was to be found, and when storms were coming. The Carrier Indians of British Columbia told New Zealand-born anthropologist Diamond Jenness that, thousands of years ago, their ancestors were married to the animals, and thus learned all they know from them. This secret knowledge, they maintain, was passed down from generation to generation and is still a living tradition today.

Certainly, the words of African shamaness Rrasebe (cited by scientist and writer Lyall Watson in his 1982 book *Lightning Bird*) encapsulate much of what the New Age movement is about: "Each of us is small and of little importance, but we are part of something far bigger. Together we belong to a system which has much power."

Life rattle
Made from painted wood trimmed with ermine, this shaman's healing rattle represents an oystercatcher, and was used by the Tlingit Indians.

school in Salerno, Italy, which was noted for accepting women. A specialist in obstetrics and gynecology, her works on the subjects remained authoritative for centuries. The need for the medical establishment to discount her on the grounds of her sex is shown clearly enough: several experts tried to suggest that Trotula was, in fact, a man.

Meanwhile, although midwifery continued to be practiced by women, it was an increasingly devalued profession, rife with superstition and secrecy. As a result, much practical knowledge fell into disuse, while spells, mumbled incantations, and amulets took precedence. A few midwives, however, still knew how to perform a cesarean section. And the common procedure of rubbing a newborn baby's skin with salt and honey may indicate some rudimentary knowledge of hygiene, since both of these substances act as mild antiseptics.

Holy women who heal

During the Middle Ages, the tradition of nuns nursing the sick evolved, and medicine and ritual became even more intricately intertwined and confused. Disease, for example, was thought to be the result of demonic possession, and touching or kissing saints' relics and reciting prayers were popularly thought to be effective cures.

At the beginning of the 16th century, the English College of Physicians openly accused women of quackery. Thomas Gale, surgeon to Queen Elizabeth I, suggested that

Merciful sisters
The traditional nun's habit is based on a style of dress popular in the Middle Ages. This mid-19th-century nun was a nurse at the Hôtel-Dieu in Paris.

Strong medicine
Watched over by an angel, a midwife assists at the birth of Samson in this 13th-century illumination.

people suffering from various diseases had been brought to that condition by "witches, by women, by counterfeit worthless fellows that take upon themselves the use of an art."

No support for women was forthcoming from the established church, to whom they were still sinful descendants of Eve, who had caused the Fall. What is more, menstruation and childbirth were thought to render them unclean, and so unfit to heal.

Yet good physicians were, as ever, in exceedingly short supply. Since all that even the best physicians could offer was purging and bleeding, people still looked to wise women for alternative treatment. In order to escape the wrath of the disapproving church, however, they received the ministrations of these women in great secrecy.

Straight from the devil?

Herbal remedies were handed down from mother to daughter. Ordinary women, prevented by law from studying medicine, and frequently illiterate in any case, relied entirely on word of mouth. Because such oral traditions were widely discounted as a viable source of knowledge, the church claimed that any skill women might possess had to have come from the devil. Thus it followed that women who were healers and midwives must be witches. Among the Latin words

The Village Doctress
A colored mezzotint after a painting by James Northcote (1746–1831) shows a healer with a cat at her feet, which may represent the traditional witch's mascot, or familiar.

used to describe witches are *herberia*, meaning one who gathers herbs, *veneficia*, poisoner, and *pixidria*, keeper of an ointment box.

Some of the botanic remedies used by these healers remain in use today. Willow bark, for instance, was often prescribed for ailments such as fevers and rheumatism. And we now know that it contains salicylic acid, otherwise known as common aspirin.

Midwives were believed to offer the babies that they delivered directly to Satan, and were therefore blamed for stillbirths, deaths during childbirth, and infant deaths of any kind. The infamous handbook on the detection and destruction of witchcraft,

Female chemistry
This 14th-century illustration depicts a female apothecary preparing medicines in an Italian pharmacy.

> "The masculine approach to illness says, 'radiate it, chemicalize it, and in general fix it through the use of your power and will.' "

the *Malleus Maleficarum* (1486), states unequivocally: "No one does more harm to the Catholic faith than midwives."

Trials and errors
For over two centuries, frenzied witch-hunts swept through Europe, then spread to North America. As a result, an estimated 200,000 people, most of them women, were brought to trial, accused of sorcery, and executed as punishment. The last official execution of witches in the United States was in 1692. Yet the role of women in traditional healing was officially limited to nursing until 1849, when an Englishwoman, Elizabeth Blackwell, graduated from Geneva (N.Y.) Medical College. She became the first woman in the United States to be

awarded an M.D. degree. At the beginning of the 1990's, nearly 150 years later, 97 percent of U.S. nurses, and only 17 percent of doctors, were female. By 2010, the American Medical Association projects that one-third of doctors will be women.

Toward a new age
Dr. Rachel Naomi Remen, Medical Director of the Commonweal Cancer Help program in Bolinas, California, has observed that "the medical system is imbalanced toward the masculine approach to illness, which says, 'radiate it, chemicalize it, and in general fix it through the use of your power and will.'" Yet the wheel is beginning to turn again, and women's traditions, knowledge, and history are now being accorded new respect by those who are committed to the alternative healing arts and their common focus on a holistic philosophy.

The green goddess
Society's concern for an ailing ecology has also made it clear that our own health and survival are irrevocably linked to the health of our planet. This awareness is very much in accord with ancient beliefs, especially those associated with the mother goddess. As Joseph Campbell writes of the Great Mother in his book *Occidental Mythology: The Masks of God:* "Even the dualism of life and death dissolves in the rapture of her solace; the worlds of nature and the spirit are not separated."

Equal signs
The increasing number of women studying medicine may help to balance the masculine and feminine approaches to healing.

EVIL ROOT
An important part of a midwife's skill was her knowledge of pain-killers. But such knowledge might encourage rumors of witchcraft, especially when the proposed remedy was mandrake, perhaps the most famous of magical plants. When dug up, the mandrake was said to utter a scream so horrible that it was deadly. To overcome this, old herbals (reference books about the medicinal properties of plants) suggested that a dog be tied to the root so that it could be pulled up safely.

We now know that there was wisdom in the use of this plant: it yields a substance called scopolamine, which has both anesthetic and sedative properties. Scopolamine is still used today to treat travel sickness and as a preoperative medication.

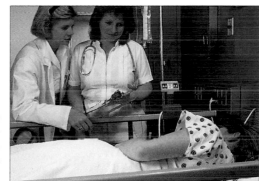

Root source
Named for its resemblance to a human body, the mandrake was thought to have human characteristics as well.

AMULETS
AND TALISMANS

Since prehistoric cave dwellers carved images in rock, people of every culture have believed in the magic healing powers of inanimate objects. These charms come in all shapes and sizes, and some of them were also believed to protect against harm and to ensure prosperity and good fortune.

Eighth-century Greek swastika

Cross purposes
The swastika is one of the world's oldest lucky charms. In its ancient form, it often represented the sun, and later became a much-valued Christian symbol. There are two kinds of swastikas: The counterclockwise version represents feminine passivity, and the clockwise form, as used in the Nazi swastika, indicates masculine energy and power.

AMULETS ARE INTENDED to ward off evil in any guise, from illness to persecution by human or demonic powers. Talismans, however, work by attracting happiness and good luck. Both can take the form of unusual objects, such as oddly shaped stones, or rare ones like four-leaf clovers. Plants and flowers are often used, as are the body parts of animals, which are thought either to encourage their characteristics (like a rabbit's foot for speed) or, in the case of dangerous animals, to protect against their attack. Relics from legendary figures are sometimes collected, and images of gods and goddesses have long been imbued with imaginary powers. Representations of male and female reproductive organs are believed to promote fertility, while some objects are valued for their color: red stones to cure blood disorders, for example, or yellow ones for jaundice.

Nazi swastika

Flower of fortune
The four-leaf clover is said to be lucky only if it is kept by its finder rather than given away. Some people believe that if an unmarried person finds one, he or she will soon meet his or her future spouse.

Birth signs
Carved from indigenous wood and reaching up to 18 inches in height, these stylized *Akuaba* figures are carried by the pregnant women of the Fanti and Ashanti tribes of Ghana in West Africa to ensure the health, beauty, and prosperity of their unborn children.

Magical elements

An almost universal charm, the horseshoe may originally have been valued for its resemblance to a crescent moon. Another theory attributes its supposed powers to its links with the blacksmith, who traditionally worked with the magical elements of iron and fire.

Warding off trouble

This wooden figure belonged to a Borneo shaman. When illness or trouble struck, he removed small chips from it in order to prepare a remedy for the sufferer.

Indian magic

This linked collection of small shaman's charms was used during the 19th century by the Tsimshian Indians of British Columbia.

Serpentine sign

In use since the third century B.C., the caduceus (an emblem consisting of two entwined snakes), is the universal symbol of Asclepius, Greek god of medicine. This silver pendant is a 20th-century copy of an 18th-century design, and was probably made in Goa (previously Portuguese India).

Snake charm

The skeleton of a snake, coiled tightly inside a copper locket, was carried as an amulet and used to ward off evil by the ancient Swedes on the island of Gotland.

Royal protection

From the tomb of the Egyptian boy-king Tutankhamen, this necklace of gold and semi-precious stones contains the left eye of Horus, a moon symbol believed to protect the dead. As was the custom, the mummy was bandaged in layers, the appropriate amulets and jewelry being placed in each layer so that the innermost held the king's personal possessions.

LIKE BY LIKE

Although we do not understand how homeopathic preparations might cure disease and alleviate chronic suffering, empirical evidence and clinical studies indicate that they do no harm and, in many cases, appear to be effective.

OPPOSING VIEWS

Samuel Christian Hahnemann called his system of medicine homeopathy, meaning "similar suffering." Conventional drug treatments he termed allopathic, from the Greek words for "different suffering," since they are designed to counteract symptoms rather than work with them. So for a patient with a high fever, a homeopath would prescribe a remedy such as aconite, derived from *Aconitum napellus,* or belladonna, which will assist the body in coping with the fever and bring it down rapidly, whereas a conventional doctor would probably recommend aspirin to lower the body's temperature by suppressing the fever.

Samuel Christian Hahnemann

HAHNEMANN.

THE SYSTEM OF MEDICINE known as homeopathy is based on the premise that an illness can be cured by a tiny amount of a medicine that produces similar symptoms in a healthy person. This principle is known as the doctrine of similars: *Similiae similibus curentur,* meaning "Let like be cured by like."

The birth of a science

Homeopathy was developed at the end of the 18th century by a respected German doctor named Samuel Christian Hahnemann (1755–1843) as a reaction against the harsh and damaging orthodox treatments of the day, such as bleeding and purging. The basis of his theory came to him in 1789 when he was translating William Cullen's *Materia Medica* (a treatise on drugs and other remedies) from English into German, and questioned Cullen's explanation for the efficacy of cinchona (Peruvian bark) in treating malaria. Cullen believed the bark's astringency to be important, but this seemed illogical to Hahnemann, since there were many remedies that were much more astringent, yet useless for malaria. Hahnemann decided to discover the effects of cinchona for himself by taking repeated doses.

Methods and means

The result of Hahnemann's experiment was dramatic: he developed symptoms very like those of malaria. Reasoning that if a drug caused the symptoms of a disease, then it might also cure it, he called his new system homeopathy, from the Greek *homoeos,* meaning "similar," and *pathos,* "suffering."

Once this principle was established, Hahnemann and his followers developed homeopathy along lines that led further and further away from medical orthodoxy. It was different in its ideas about preventing illness, in its methods of diagnosis, and in its treatments, which involved selecting and preparing medicines in exact and unusual ways.

In homeopathic diagnosis, for example, the emphasis is on working with the symptoms the patient is able to describe in addition to discovering the underlying disease, and on accomplishing both without the use of extensive — and often intrusive — tests. Unusual symptoms that do not fit the accepted picture of an illness may be even more important than the more common symptoms, because homeopathy is highly individualized. What may be appropriate for one person with a given disease will not work for someone else.

Initially, the patient is asked about his or her personality, general disposition and state of mind; his or her likes and dislikes in everything from food to weather, and particular sensitivities and aversions. Apart from determining precise symptoms, questions will

This principle is known as the doctrine of similars: *Similiae similibus curentur*, meaning "Let like be cured by like."

establish things like the conditions that affect these symptoms, and the exact nature of any pain. From the roughly 2,000 medicines available, one is chosen that matches the patient's profile, complete with the symptoms they are experiencing. This process is called repertorizing, after the repertory, or homeopathic symptom index, which is now available as a computer database as well as in book form.

Living proof
Every drug "picture" in the homeopathic *materia medica* has been arrived at by "proving" — testing it on a healthy person to ascertain the symptoms it produces. This is simply an extension of Samuel Hahnemann's original method of trying remedies on himself. Additional information about homeopathic drugs is also gleaned from toxicology (the study of poisons) and from documented clinical cures.

These drugs may be of vegetable, mineral, or animal origin, and can even be taken from disease discharge, such as pus. Some plant remedies have a history of medicinal use, while others, like *Arsenicum album* (arsenic), are, quite literally, poisons. Whatever their origins, however, all substances become homeopathic medicines only by a unique method known as serial dilution and succussion, which produces what are called "potentized" remedies.

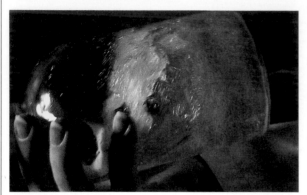

Shaken, not stirred
The succussion (shaking) involved in producing homeopathic remedies can be done by hand or machine.

STARTLING STATISTICS

In 1854, when cholera spread throughout Europe, the London Homoeopathic Hospital, along with many others, devoted its wards to the treatment of cholera victims. The records of what was then the Board of Health show a dramatic difference in mortality rates between hospitals. While the average mortality was about 60 percent, the Homoeopathic Hospital reportedly lost only around 16 percent of its patients. Significantly, homeopathic physician Frederick Foster Quin, supported by his influential friend Lord Ebury, had to fight in order to have these statistics recorded.

Death's dispensary
In this contemporary illustration, the cholera epidemic of the mid-19th century is shown to have its origins in the highly polluted water supply.

In the case of liquids, this is accomplished by soaking an extract of the substance in a solution of alcohol to form the "mother tincture," which is then diluted with alcohol in ratios of one drop of tincture to 10 or 100 drops of alcohol. This is shaken vigorously or succussed, a technique described by Hahnemann as a "rubbing and shaking," which he believed to bring about a quality change. Similarly, solids are diluted by being repeatedly titurated (rubbed or ground) with lactose and sucrose, using a mortar and pestle, then eventually formed into tablets. "The power to heal is released," he said, "so that even a totally inert substance can come to influence the vital force." These procedures are repeated to achieve a range of different potencies, sometimes to a point well beyond what is known as Avogadro's number (named after the 19th-century Italian chemist and physicist Amedeo Avogadro), which means that not one molecule of the original substance is left. In fact, homeopathic practitioners have found that the more diluted the solution is, the more effective the remedy proves.

Homeopathic treatment is guided by two principles. The first holds that only one remedy at a time should be given by the homeopath, who should observe its effect before considering

> ### "The power to heal is released," he said, "so that even a totally inert substance can come to influence the vital force."

whether further medication is called for. The second principle is that the dosage should be minimal. Then if the patient has been prescribed the correct remedy at the appropriate potency, healing should begin. This process may be signaled by a temporary worsening of the symptoms, known as homeopathic aggravation. This phase should soon be followed by one of rapid improvement.

Principles of prescription

If the remedy given proves to be wrong, however, and produces a severe reaction, Hahnemann advised that an "antidote must be administered." If the reactions "are not too violent," he recommended, "the correct remedy must be given immediately." Regarding the recommended potencies and the suggested length of treatment, he stated that "the degree of every dose must deviate somewhat from the preceding and following doses." In this way, some remedies may be given daily for a period of months. If the medicine does not fully restore health, Hahnemann concluded: "We examine again and again the diseased state that remains, selecting each time a homeopathic medicine as suitable as possible until health is accomplished."

As a result, homeopathy may not be a speedy process. Some practitioners believe that a month of treatment is needed for every year of illness suffered. Nevertheless it can be — and often is — used for relief of acute complaints, such as asthma, and is also of value as a preventive, since remedies may be prescribed in order to deter inherent weaknesses from developing into chronic conditions in later life.

Home remedies

Homeopathic medicines are available over the counter as well as from specialist practitioners. About 50 commonly used remedies are sold in low-potency forms to deal with day-to-day problems such as bruises, headache, fever, and stomach upsets.

Homeopathy may function outside the realm of orthodox medicine, but historical records, laboratory research, clinical trials, and case studies done by homeopaths, medical doctors, and veterinary surgeons, offer a seemingly impressive array of evidence to suggest that it does work. For example, a trial study at Glasgow University involving hay fever sufferers carried out in the late 1980's (and evaluated by the University of Glasgow's departments of statistics and immunology) showed that people given a homeopathic preparation had six times fewer symptoms than those given a placebo. Yet homeopaths are doubtful that such findings will be accepted by the scientific community. This is because they are aware of the power of orthodox medical politics, having seen homeopathy in its short history reduced from a popular, thriving profession to near extinction, especially in many parts of the United States.

Homeopathy under siege

After homeopathy was introduced to the U.S. in 1825 by the Dutch homeopath Hans Gram, the number of practitioners increased rapidly. In 1844 they formed the first national medical society, the American Institute of Homeopathy. Two years later the American Medical Association (AMA) was established. In its charter, the AMA refused to admit either state or local medical groups to its ranks unless they agreed to ban all homeopaths. But homeopathy continued to grow and prosper. By 1900 there were 22 homeopathic medical schools, more than 100 hospitals, and over 1,000 pharmacies.

Finally, in 1910, the Carnegie Foundation, in cooperation with the AMA, produced a report on medical schools (the Flexner Report) which gave low ratings to homeopathic colleges. Unfortunately for such schools, the report became the basis on which medical education was organized; so it gave the AMA the necessary grounds on which to refuse licenses to homeopathic graduates. As a result, attendance at schools dropped, and since these institutions, unlike their orthodox counterparts, were given no government support, their numbers dwindled. By 1923 there were only two colleges in the United States that still taught homeopathy.

A new lease of life?

Since 1970, however, there has been a remarkable resurgence of interest in homeopathy, the first since the decline at the beginning of the century. There are eight homeopathic academies in different parts of the U.S., and several states now recognize practitioners. More and more M.D.'s are also qualifying in homeopathy, and a number of clinics have been established (such as the very successful one in Berkeley, California). It is too soon to say, however, whether the popularity of this gentle, natural, and holistic medical system will continue to grow, or whether it will eventually wither under the continuous criticisms of the orthodox medical community.

Hysterical attack
The bite of the wolf spider (Lycosa tarentula) was once thought to produce hallucinations and hysteria; its venom contains a substance, also called Tarentula, that is used by homeopaths to treat fits and some psychological conditions.

Pills and potions
Homeopathic medicines can be stored in their bottles indefinitely in a cool, dark place. But if they are handled, or come into contact with any kind of strong perfume or scent, practitioners believe that they may lose some or all of their potency.

NATURAL IMMUNITY

Often perceived as being diametrically opposed to homeopathy, orthodox medicine actually shares with it some types of treatment. The principle of vaccination, for example, has something in common with the basis of homeopathy – that is, treating like with like. In fact, Samuel Hahnemann made his original discovery about the same time that English physician Edward Jenner was experimenting with inoculations of matter drawn from cowpox lesions to immunize against smallpox.

Prevention and cure

The essential difference between the two is that immunization seeks to prevent disease through the injection of altered or killed toxins or infectious organisms similar or identical to those involved in a disease. These encourage the body's immune system to produce antibodies and thus fight off the infection. Homeopathy, however, attempts to cure illness using natural remedies that, if given in large quantities, would cause symptoms in a healthy person similar to those of the patient.

CURING THE FAMOUS

From O. J. Simpson to Tina Turner, there is an impressive list of people who have depended on homeopathic remedies to cure illness and maintain health.

John D. Rockefeller, Sr.
The philanthropic oil magnate referred to homeopathy as "a progressive and aggressive step in medicine." Under homeopathic care throughout his later years, he lived to be 99.

The duchess of Teck and Princess Victoria Mary
Britain's royal family have favored homeopathic treatments for generations. The foundation stone of the present London Homoeopathic Hospital was laid in 1893 by the duchess of Teck and her daughter Princess Victoria Mary of Teck, who later married King George V and became Queen Mary. The present queen's father, George VI, used homeopathy to cure his severe seasickness.

FROM THE TIME OF ITS DEVELOPMENT by Samuel Christian Hahnemann at the end of the 18th century, the system of healing known as homeopathy has proved popular with well-known and successful people from every walk of life.

In the field of literature, such distinguished writers as Charles Dickens, Louisa May Alcott, Nathaniel Hawthorne, Henry Wadsworth Longfellow, and W. B. Yeats all took homeopathic medicines.

A wide range of entertainers, from the composer and pianist Frédéric Chopin to 20th-century stars such as Sir Laurence Olivier, Sir Yehudi Menuhin, Lindsay Wagner, and Tina Turner, have relied on Hahnemann's preparations to deal with conditions such as exhaustion, stage fright, voice weakness, and jet lag.

Sporting chances

One area in which homeopathy is particularly popular is sport: A significant number of famous athletes depend on it not only to relieve injuries, but also to improve their general health and fitness, and therefore their performance. Among these are the former football star, running back O. J. Simpson, ex-Yankee pitcher Jim Bouton (who deals with his serious asthma using homeopathy), basketball coach Pat Riley, professional golfer Sally Little, and Kate Schmidt, the U.S. Olympic medalist in javelin throwing. Arnica, a preparation used to alleviate shock, sore muscles, and bruising, is probably the most common homeopathic remedy employed by sports figures.

Sir John Weir
Appointed physician to King George V and Queen Mary, homeopathic practitioner Sir John Weir continued in this role until his retirement at the end of the 1960's. He was replaced as royal physician by another homeopathic specialist, Dr. Marjorie Blackie.

Tina Turner
Singer Tina Turner testified to her belief in homeopathy, both in her autobiography *I, Tina* and in an interview she gave to *Vogue* magazine in May 1985.

Mark Twain

The author of *Tom Sawyer* (shown here in a portrait painted by J. M. Flagg) expressed a typically blunt opinion of the medical climate of his day. "The introduction of homeopathy," Mark Twain wrote in an 1890 issue of *Harper's Magazine,* "forced the old school doctor to stir around and learn something of a rational nature about his business."

Mahatma Gandhi

The Indian statesman (shown with his granddaughters in New Delhi) was a firm believer in homeopathy, and his support increased its popularity in his country. Homeopathic doctors claim that Hahnemann's remedies are particularly effective in treating the infectious diseases and chronic conditions widespread in India, and they cost much less than conventional drugs, making them more easily available to the generally poor population.

Queen Victoria and Prince Albert

The marriage of Albert and Victoria in 1840 ensured the popularity of homeopathy in the British royal family, since it was Albert's aunt, Queen Adelaide, wife of the British king William IV (1765–1837), who first encouraged its use by members of the royal household.

Yehudi Menuhin

This internationally renowned violinist has been quoted as stating: "Homeopathy is one of the few medical specialties that carries no penalties — only benefits." His strong support is reflected in the fact that he is president of the Hahnemann Society, a major, international homeopathic organization.

CHAPTER TWO

THE POWER OF BELIEF

Mind-programming that seems to permit surgery without anesthetic, inactive "drugs" that may heal cancer, hypnotic suggestion that relieves severe burns, religious faith that produces "miracle cures" — all involve the amazing power of the mind over the body.

At the Hospital of the Virgin of the Beautiful Water Meadows in Murcia, Spain, Dr. Angel Escudero regularly performs or supervises surgical operations carried out without anesthetic. Before surgery, Escudero invites the patient to do two things. One is to program his or her brain, as if it were a computer, to instruct the body to protect itself in whatever way is required. The other is to keep the mouth moist with saliva. This startlingly simple procedure seems to work for Escudero's patients as effectively as modern medical techniques.

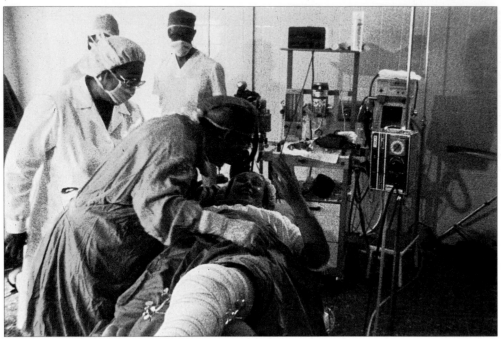

Painless surgery
Dr. Angel Escudero congratulates his sister after her successful leg operation. It was performed without anesthetic, using "noesitherapy," a pain-control technique pioneered by Escudero.

The patient lay fully conscious on the operating table, chatting to her sister-in-law, while the surgeon opened the skin of her lower leg, sawed away part of one bone, drilled holes in another, and inserted metal rods through it.

The doctor calls his method "noesitherapy," from the Greek *noesis* (meaning "action of thinking").

In 1991 a BBC science program showed Escudero supervising an operation on his sister, Marie Magdalena, in front of several orthodox doctors. The surgery, carried out by Dr. Carlos Clavel, an orthopedic specialist, was designed to repair her bowed leg bones that had led, over the years, to arthritis. The patient lay fully conscious, chatting to her sister-in-law, while the surgeon opened the skin of her lower leg, sawed away part of one bone, drilled holes in another, and inserted metal rods through it. Marie Magdalena, who had not even been given a local anesthetic, reported only "very pleasant sensations," and her pulse rate remained low and stable.

Following the operation, the program showed Escudero in conversation with several orthodox doctors, including Dr. F Payadore, a Spanish psychiatry and neurophysiology specialist. Payadore suggested that although Escudero's pain-control method had appeared to work on this and other occasions, accurate scientific analysis would need to be performed before noesitherapy would be accepted by the medical community.

Immune to infection
Not only do Dr. Escudero's patients apparently feel no pain, but reportedly they recover faster than people subjected to normal surgery under anesthetics, and never suffer post-operative infections.

Evidence of the power of the mind over the body, for instance to control pain, has not always been accepted by the medical establishment. For example, when working in India in the 1940's, the British physician James Esdaile reported using hypnosis to perform many painless surgical operations. However, attempts by doctors in other countries to replicate his work failed, and his results were regarded as inconclusive. Today, the medical profession has a different view of the relationship between mind and body. Most doctors now agree that a person's mental attitude can have a great influence not only on the perception of pain but also on the possibility of falling ill and the chances for recovery.

The power of the placebo
Probably the most thoroughly researched phenomenon that demonstrates the power of the mind over pain and sickness is the "placebo effect." For many years doctors have observed that placebos (inactive substances administered to patients) often prove as effective as active medication. Before the 1970's, when the ethics of using placebos on unsuspecting patients were questioned, thousands of tests were conducted in which a placebo was substituted for aspirin or morphine to relieve pain. In more than a third of cases the placebo appeared to be as effective as the painkiller. It is interesting to note that those who thought they were being given morphine experienced greater pain relief than those who thought they were taking aspirin.

There is nothing new about the placebo effect. In the late 18th century people with toothache were advised to crush a worm between finger and thumb of the right hand and to touch the painful tooth with the pulp. A follow-up study of this intriguing but medically groundless technique reported that it relieved toothache in 431 cases out of 629.

▶ PAGE 48

EXERCISING CONTROL

Many body processes, such as heart rate and blood pressure, are considered to be involuntary. Yet biofeedback techniques have enabled some patients to control these functions and so improve their health.

PIONEERED IN THE 1950's AND 1960's, a medical technique known as biofeedback has helped many people suffering from stress-related illnesses. These include migraine and tension headaches, abnormal heart rhythms, asthma, some forms of epilepsy, and various nervous diseases.

The technique works in the following way. The doctor connects the patient to a special instrument that monitors a particular body process, such as heart rate, brain wave fluctuations, blood pressure, or muscle tension. Changes in the monitoring signals then keep the patient informed of changes in his or her body processes (this is what is known as biofeedback). The monitoring signal may be a flashing light, a needle on a dial, or an audible tone. As treatment progresses, the patient is taught to become aware, whenever the signal changes, of a corresponding change in how he or she feels — for example, more tense or more relaxed.

Monitoring the body
Gradually the patient learns how to consciously change the way he or she feels and thus to regulate the signal — and the body process being monitored. For example, someone with an irregular heart rhythm may be taught, by means of biofeedback relayed by colored-light signals, how to stabilize the heart rate. Eventually the patient may be able to control the body function without using the biofeedback machine and so gain control of his or her condition.

Pioneering work was done in the 1960's by the neuropsychiatrist Dr. Joe Kamiya at the University of Chicago.

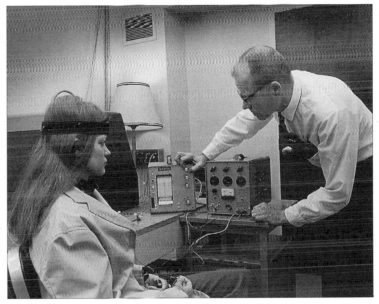
Wired for brain-wave training
Dr. Green prepares a patient at the Menninger Clinic in Topeka, Kansas.

Using an electroencephalograph (EEG) machine, which measures brain waves, Kamiya taught subjects to recognize when their brain was producing alpha waves. These are the waves characteristic of a person who is relaxed and content. By means of a changing tone, the subjects then learned how to turn on the alpha state — that is, to relax at will.

A treatment for epilepsy
In their book *Beyond Biofeedback* (1977), Elmer and Alyce Green report how brain-wave biofeedback training can help some epileptics. Using the technique such patients are sometimes able to produce beneficial brain waves and so reduce the frequency of seizures.

At Harvard University in the 1960's psychology professor Gary E. Schwartz carried out extensive studies on subjects given audio feedback on their heart rate and blood pressure. When the subjects were able to lower both factors together, they reported feeling calm and peaceful.

Nonetheless, biofeedback is not in itself a cure for illness. Yet there is little doubt that, together with other forms of relaxation therapy, it may act as a preventive, and may help improve the patient's state of well-being.

Biofeedback indicator
This instrument is designed to show the depth of a subject's meditation.

HEALING BY SUGGESTION

The father of the modern medical use of hypnosis is considered to be the Scottish surgeon James Braid (1795–1860). In the early 1840's, before the introduction of anesthetics, Braid successfully used hypnotism to reduce pain during surgery.

After Braid died, hypnotism was neglected by the medical profession until the 1880's, when the French neurologist Jean-Martin Charcot (1825–93) claimed that hysterical paralysis, deafness, and blindness could be induced and removed by hypnosis. This claim proved false, but medical interest in the subject had been revived.

Relieving pain

Today, with powerful painkilling drugs available, it might be thought that hypnosis no longer has a role to play in pain relief. But this is not so. In 1988 R. John Wakeman of the Ochsner Clinic in New Orleans reported that people in an experimental group of burn victims who received hypnosis as part of their therapy

did better at tolerating heat at work (such as outdoor work in summer) than a control group of burn victims who were not hypnotized. Three years later, 20 out of 25 in the control group had left their jobs because they could not bear heat, while only two of those who had been hypnotized had done so.

In 1982 Howard R. Hall, a psychologist at Pennsylvania State University, reported on his findings concerning hypnosis, the immune system, and cancer. One finding was that certain hypnotized people can somehow consciously increase the

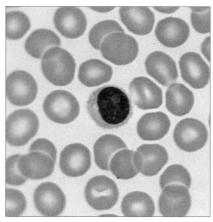

Protective blood cell
A special type of blood cell that increases the body's resistance to disease, known as a lymphocyte, can be seen here nestling among ordinary red blood cells.

production of white blood cells in their body. Some white cells, known as lymphocytes, are crucial to the immune system. An increase in their number not only helps to protect against the development of cancer but also helps in the fight against an existing tumor.

Curing addictions

Hypnosis is also used to help various emotional difficulties. In psychoanalysis a patient may be hypnotized to induce him or her to live through, and come to terms with, past experiences that have been repressed. Addictions can also be treated. Hypnotherapists claim that they need only three to five sessions to stop a patient smoking or start one losing weight.

Jean-Martin Charcot

Psychosomatic illness

It has long been known that some disorders, such as asthma, migraine headache, and stomach ulcers, may be stress-related. These illnesses have been called psychosomatic, from the Greek *psyche* (meaning "soul" or "mind") and *soma* (meaning "body"). Recent research has shown that certain people who are lonely, anxious, grief-stricken, or otherwise subjected to stress may be more susceptible to a variety of illnesses. These include diabetes, tuberculosis, heart disease, and even cancer.

In 1989 Dr. Amanda Ramirez of Guy's Hospital, London, found that severe stress made a relapse more likely among women who had recovered from breast cancer. The women who had relapses were compared to a control group of breast cancer patients who remained well. Dr. Ramirez found that the sick women were nine times more likely to have experienced severe stress just before their cancers recurred.

Controlling the system

In the search for a key to psychosomatic illness, a new medical discipline has evolved — psychoneuroimmunology (PNI). The discipline deals with the links between the brain and the immune system, the cells and proteins that form the main line of defense against disease.

Until recently it was thought that the immune system worked independently of the brain. But then in the 1970's Robert Ader, a psychologist at the University of Rochester, accidentally conditioned rats to suppress their own immune system functions, causing them to become sick. He then succeeded in conditioning them to modulate their immune responses.

The effects of stress

This led medical scientists to wonder whether in humans, too, the mind might exert control over the immune system. Since then, neuroscientists such as Karen Bulloch at the University of California at San Diego have carried out research that indicates that the mind probably does have, if not control, then at the least, some form of influence. When a person is under stress, for example, the brain appears to release hormones that inhibit the activity of the immune system.

Party therapy
Harold H. Benjamin, founder of the Wellness Community, at one of the social gatherings the members consider important to maintain health.

Dr. Michael Antoni, of the University of Miami, conducted an investigation into whether or not the mind might help to slow the progression of the AIDS virus, which attacks the immune system. During a 10 week study, it became apparent that groups of HIV-positive patients that were given aerobic, relaxation, and assertiveness training showed less signs of depression and anxiety than a group that received no training. At the end of the study, the trained groups also appeared to have healthier immune systems.

Keeping AIDS at bay

Dr. Antoni said: "With HIV infection there's a steady decline in immune status. Perhaps by changing the contribution that distress makes to the formula, we can keep the immune system to a slower decline or possibly no decline at all. Then when pharmaceutical regimens become available, the person will be able to benefit from those. So we're talking here about a holding pattern, in what has previously been seen as a progressive disease."

Some doctors feel that the depression caused by isolation harms the immune system and contributes to early death. In 1982 the Wellness Community was founded to help counter this problem.

With headquarters in Santa Monica, California, and 10 facilities in four states, the community uses groups led by psychotherapists and "camaraderie, togetherness and support" to supplement conventional cancer treatment.

During the 1980's there was great interest in PNI and mind-body interactions. This led Dr. Steven Locke of the Beth Israel Hospital in Boston to speak of this new activity as a "third revolution" in modern medicine — the first two were the development of surgery and the discovery of penicillin.

Dr. Herbert Benson, of Boston's New England Deaconess Hospital, shows his patients how to meditate to counter pain

---

Now the medical profession generally accepts that the attitude of the doctor is important in combating illness.

---

and aid recovery. Cancer patients are taught to visualize the destruction of the malignant cells in their bodies.

Once there was an unbridgable gulf between the "healer," who cured through a direct, close relationship with the sufferer, and the detached doctor, who cured through diagnosis and treatment. Now the medical profession generally accepts that the attitude of the doctor is important in combating illness.

An emotional approach

In his bestselling book, *Love, Medicine and Miracles* (1986), Connecticut cancer specialist Dr. Bernie S. Siegel described what happened after he switched from conventional treatment to therapy based on an emotional relationship between doctor and patient. He wrote: "People whose conditions had been stable or deteriorating for a long time suddenly began to get well before my eyes."

One of the most extraordinary examples of the power of belief over illness concerns a cancer patient. The story was recounted by psychologist Bruno Klopfer in an address to a medical society in 1957. A man whom Klopfer referred to as Mr. Wright was suffering from an advanced stage of cancer. He had "huge tumor masses, the size of oranges...in the neck, axillas [armpits], groins, chest and abdomen." The physician treating him, Dr. Philip West, decided to administer an injection of Krebiozen, much publicized at the time as a wonder cure for cancer. The effect was dramatic — the tumors quickly shrank to half their original size. However, Mr. Wright then came across some newspaper reports that cast doubt on the drug's effectiveness. He immediately suffered a relapse.

Little white lie
Desperate to save his patient, Dr. West resorted to deception. He persuaded Wright that Krebiozen really did work, and gave him what he claimed was a double-strength injection of the drug, although the syringe contained nothing but water. Over the next two months, Wright, once more believing in the cure, began to recover again.

Deprived of faith
But the doctor's stratagem was subverted by a final blow: the American Medical Association reported that tests proved Krebiozen to be valueless as a treatment. Within days of this announcement, Wright was dead. Deprived of the faith and hope that the drug had inspired, he apparently could no longer sustain his fight against the disease.

The healing spring
A paralyzed man seeks a cure in the supposedly healing waters of St. Winefride's Well, Holywell, Clwyd, in Wales.

A HIGHER POWER

Throughout history there have been reports of sick people who have healed themselves through the power of their religious belief. This is said to occur as a result of fervent prayer, a visit to a shrine, or a holy person's touch. There are some similar cases, however, that involve no faith of any kind.

Jesus and the sick woman
This 19th-century stained-glass window in the Royal Infirmary, Lancaster, England, depicts one of the best-known examples of faith healing in the Bible.

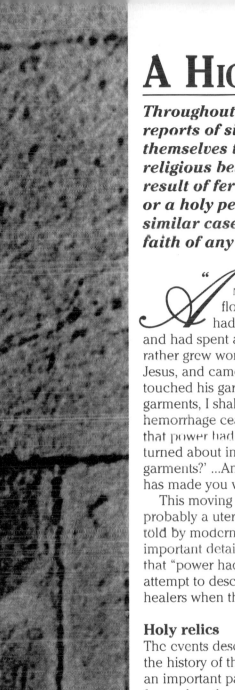

"AND THERE WAS A WOMAN who had had a flow of blood for twelve years, and who had suffered much under many physicians, and had spent all that she had, and was no better but rather grew worse. She had heard the reports about Jesus, and came up behind him in the crowd and touched his garment. For she said, 'If I touch even his garments, I shall be made well.' And immediately the hemorrhage ceased....And Jesus, perceiving in himself that power had gone forth from him, immediately turned about in the crowd, and said, 'Who touched my garments?' ...And he said to her, 'Daughter, your faith has made you well....'" (Mark 5:25 – 34)

This moving account of a woman with what was probably a uterine hemorrhage being cured is often told by modern-day believers in faith healing. One important detail it mentions is Jesus' immediate sense that "power had gone forth from him." This is an attempt to describe a feeling that is common to most healers when they exercise their gift.

Holy relics

The events described in The Acts of the Apostles and the history of the early church show that healing was an important part of early Christian practice. The favored method was the laying on of hands — the healer touching the diseased part of the sufferer. Paul, however, suggested that healing was a special gift not given to all believers. In 1 Corinthians 12:8 – 9, he says: "To one is given through the Spirit the utterance of wisdom...to another faith...to another gifts of healing."

By the 10th century it was widely believed that simply touching holy relics, such as the bones of dead saints and martyrs, might effect a cure. Eventually this was to lead to the peddling of fake relics. But most of the early shrines did indeed contain genuine remains. In France, Spain, and Italy, many of these shrines continue to attract pilgrims to this day.

Miracle cures

The Roman Catholic Church, however, has laid down strict criteria as to what constitutes a miraculous cure. These include the following: the cure must be impossible to reproduce by known medical treatment;

> "And Jesus, perceiving in himself that power had gone forth from him, immediately turned about in the crowd, and said, 'Who touched my garments?'...And he said to her, 'Daughter, your faith has made you well....' "
> (Mark 5:25 – 34)

Healing mask

A mask from Sri Lanka used in the treatment of diseases. The mask is used to help the afflicted person visualize his or her particular malaise in order to cure it.

it must be instant and complete; and there must be no relapse.

Any cure that does not meet the above criteria but is brought about by prayer or by visiting a shrine is known as a faith cure. The church has given cautious approval to various shrines claimed to effect faith cures. These include La Salette, in France; Knock, in Ireland; Beauraing, in Belgium; and Fatima, in Portugal.

Claimed miracle cures are largely confined to Lourdes, a town in the French Pyrenees. It was there, at 12:30 P.M. on February 11, 1858, that a 14-year-old girl named Bernadette Soubirous claimed that she had seen the Virgin Mary in a grotto. There were several more reports of visitations, during some of which Bernadette was accompanied to the grotto by church officials. They were unable to see the apparition, but noticed that, while apparently in a trance, the girl cupped her hands over a flame without burning herself.

Within months visitors to the grotto were reporting that their illnesses were being miraculously cured. Four years later a church commission decided that Bernadette's visions were genuine.

Medical notes

Today the sick are examined on arrival at the shrine and are expected to produce signed medical notes about their condition. If a cure is reported, a church medical board examines the person. Particularly impressive cases are forwarded to an even higher medical bureau and an ecclesiastical tribunal, which decides whether or not a genuine miracle cure has taken place.

Between 1858 and the present day millions of pilgrims have visited Lourdes. By the 1980's some three million people a year were flocking to the grotto. However, in all that time less than 60 cures have been judged to be

THE STROKER

In 1662 Valentine Greatrakes (1629–83), an Irish landowner, had what he described as "an impulse or strange persuasion to heal" by the laying on of hands. This was odd since he admitted to being squeamish about wounds and sores; his wife dismissed the idea as nonsense. But Greatrakes followed his urge and was soon reportedly healing "deafness, blindness, cancers, sciatica, palsies...and the like."

The bishop of Dromore recorded that "something healing, something balsamic" flowed from The

Valentine Greatrakes

Stroker, as Greatrakes was called. One contemporary, Dr. Astel, said: "I saw Greatrakes in a moment remove most violent pains merely by his hand."

A change of heart

The celebrated chemist Robert Boyle and various other members of the Royal Society testified to the authenticity of Greatrakes's cures. But after a few years he gave up his healing and quietly withdrew to his estate. He had decided that he was not comfortable with the attention his unusual gift had brought him.

miraculous. And even these have been regarded with skepticism by medical doctors. In the 1960's, for example, the English psychiatrist Dr. D. J. West, noted for his work in psychical research, examined 11 "miracle" cures acclaimed since 1947 and found flaws in the evidence for each one. He suggested setting up a center for controlled studies in Lourdes. "In the absence of a research team investigating whole groups of pilgrims," wrote Dr. West, "one cannot be sure that a special curative factor exists, much less find out how it works."

Essential life force

The idea that certain places and people have the ability to channel some kind of healing power existed long before the miracles of Christ. Five centuries before, Sanskrit texts were describing Indian

> ## "The heat which oozes out of the hand, on being applied to the sick, is highly salutary."
>
> ### Hippocrates

techniques for harnessing *prana* (the essential life force) for healing, both by the laying on of hands and by meditation. The Chinese called the same power *chi*, believing it to flow through the body along certain lines that might be blocked or cleared. These concepts survive today and form the basis of yoga and acupuncture respectively.

Drawing out evil

The aborigines of Australia and tribal peoples of several African countries use apparently successful healing techniques in which a patient is touched by a spear or a wand while incantations are recited by a holy man. The object is to draw out the evil spirits that are believed to be the root cause of all illnesses.

Successful laying on of hands is not, however, necessarily dependent on religious faith, Christian or otherwise. The Greek physician Hippocrates (*c.*460–*c.*377 B.C.), generally regarded as the father of medicine, noted that "just as

HEALING FROM AFAR

Requested by the church to cease healing by laying on of hands, a 19th-century German priest found that he had the power to cure people at a distance — even thousands of miles away.

SINCE THE REFORMATION the Roman Catholic Church has frowned upon faith-healing priests. But in the case of the priestly German prince, Father von Hohenlohe, there was little the church could do about his healing activities.

Born near Waldenburg in 1794 — as Alexander Leopold Franz Emmerick, prince von Hohenlohe-Waldenburg-Schillings-Furst — von Hohenlohe was a particularly devout child. At the age of 27, after having been a Catholic priest for some years, von Hohenlohe discovered that he had healing powers. He is reported to have cured the sick by the laying on of hands, by praying with them, or simply by ordering them to be well.

Prominent social position

Because of von Hohenlohe's aristocratic background and social position, his cures became widely known, and both the church and the German medical authorities pleaded with him to abandon his healing. To placate them, the priest took up instead what he called absent healing. He let it be known that at certain hours of the day, at his church in Bamberg, Bavaria, he would offer up prayers and Mass for the sick. He asked those who were ill to pray at the same times, and to write to him if they required any specific prayers.

By these means, von Hohenlohe was said to have brought about some celebrated cures. One well-attested case, in 1822, was that of a nun, Barbara O'Connor, resident in a convent near Chelmsford, England.

Father von Hohenlohe

According to Dr. John Badeley, who attended the nun and who wrote a pamphlet on her case the following year, she had suffered from a painful, swollen, immovable arm for 18 months. Doctors had tried many treatments without success. On the day that Father von Hohenlohe prayed for Sister O'Connor, "the pain instantly left her, and the swelling gradually subsided." A few weeks later she was completely cured.

Deathbed recovery

An even more widely publicized case occurred less than two years later in the U.S. Mrs. Mastingly, the sister of Thomas Carbury, the mayor of Washington, D.C., was terminally ill and had asked for the prayers of von Hohenlohe. At 3:30 P.M. on March 20, 1824, Mass was celebrated at the sick woman's bedside, coinciding with one at the German priest's church. The following account is taken from the *Catholic Spectator*: "At the moment of receiving the Blessed Sacrament...she rises up in her bed, and lifting up her two arms, one of which she had not been able for a long time even to move, she exclaims: 'Lord Jesus, what have I done to obtain so great a favor?'...' asks for her clothes, dresses herself, sits up, throws herself down on her knees with the priest the Rev. Stephen Dubuisson...who was prostrate on the ground, lost in a transport of admiration and gratitude, then rises, walks through the room, and on that morning took as much food as she had taken for the space of six months previous."

some diseases may be communicated from one to another," so "health may be imparted in the sick by certain gestures, and by contact...the heat which oozes out of the hand, on being applied to the sick, is highly salutary."

In the 1880's, during a visit to the U.S., the English scientist F. W. Myers and an American colleague observed a doctor

using hand-healing on his patients. Impressed, Myers's colleague asked to have a minor ailment of his own treated. The doctor snorted and shook his head emphatically. "Sorry," he said, "it just don't work on educated folks."

Therapeutic Touch

Perhaps the doctor should have given it a try. A century later, in the 1970's, Dolores Krieger, professor emeritus of nursing at New York University, found that hand-healing improved the condition of a number of her patients. As a result, Krieger taught nurses to use the technique as part of treatment. In Krieger's version of the therapy, known as Therapeutic Touch (TT), the hands do not make actual contact with the sick person's body but merely hover above it, "specifically directing the healing energy." Krieger suggests that TT is particularly beneficial in cases of musculoskeletal and psychosomatic disorders: she says that patients feel more relaxed, suffer less pain, and recover more quickly.

Perking up the president

Among the least likely people to experience and vouch for the curative properties of hand-healing might be the late president of the Soviet Union, Leonid Brezhnev. In the winter of 1979 Brezhnev was visibly ailing: his gait was shambling, his speech slurred. But by spring 1980 he was a changed man. According to Craig R. Whitney, Moscow correspondent of *The New York Times*, the cure had been wrought by an ex-waitress from the Soviet state of Georgia, Dzhuna Davitashvili, who had also treated other ministers at her Moscow apartment. Interviewed by writer Henry Gris, Davitashvili claimed that "bioenergy" streaming from her palms was the secret of her cures.

Mexican faith healing

A ceremony of healing and penance at the village of Espinazo, in northern Mexico, is held annually in memory of the late faith healer "El Niño" Fidencio Constantino, who died in October 1938. Here a materia, *or guide, immerses a follower in the water of a local pool to cleanse him of his sins. Local children are also baptized in this pool.*

TUNING INTO THE DIVINE MIND

*To Christian Scientists sickness is nothing more than a variant of sin —
an "error" of the mortal mind. They believe that physical well-being can
be attained only by entering into harmony with the divine mind.*

THE CHRISTIAN SCIENCE RELIGIOUS MOVEMENT was the
first organized attempt to deal with the problem
of physical disease through purely spiritual
means. Its founder was the Boston-born Mary Baker
Eddy (1821–1910), but its roots go back to the
pioneering work of the German physician
Franz Anton Mesmer (1734–1815).

Mesmer, who practiced in Paris,
believed that "the magnetic influence
of the heavens" affected the body.
Sickness was caused by an
interruption in the course of this
magnetism, he theorized. Healing
consisted in restoring its ebb and flow.
This was done by a combination of
"magnetic" touch and a primitive
form of hypnosis (which was
known as mesmerism).

Animal magnetism
Mesmer's theory, dubbed "animal
magnetism," became immensely
popular. One of its most ardent
followers in the U.S. was Phineas Quimby,
a clockmaker of Portland, Maine. Quimby
discovered that, partly by using techniques based on
Mesmer's and partly by employing gentle suggestion, he
was able to heal the sick. In 1862 one of his visitors was
41-year-old Mrs. Mary Patterson (later to be widowed
and remarry as Mrs. Mary Baker
Eddy). She was crippled with
spinal problems that conventional
medicine had been unable to
ease. Quimby reportedly managed
to cure her completely.

A profound experience
Impressed, Eddy studied Quimby's
and Mesmer's healing methods
and integrated them with her own
fundamentalist Christian beliefs.
Then, four years later, she
underwent a profoundly moving
experience. While convalescing
from severe injuries sustained in a
fall, she was reading her Bible.
When she read about Jesus' raising of the palsied man,
God's presence suddenly seemed to flood her whole
being, and she too rose from her bed healed.

Mary Baker Eddy

This remarkable recovery inspired Eddy to develop her
own theory of sickness and healing. Its basic tenet is
that disease is linked to "errors" of the mortal mind,
namely fear, ignorance, and sin. According to her
system, healing comes when the errors of the
mortal mind are cast out by the giving of
oneself to the divine mind, or God.

A new church
In 1875 Eddy published her theory under
the title *Science and Health with Key to the
Scriptures.* Four years later in Boston she
established the Church of Christ, Scientist,
whose doctrine is based on the teachings
of Christ. The movement flourished and,
despite its shunning of publicity, there
are now some 2,700 Christian Science
churches in various countries
around the world.

Christian Scientists reject
orthodox medicine totally — not
only drugs but even such simple
measures as ice packs. One Christian
Science publication put the philosophy
like this: "What needs to be healed is always
a false concept of being, not a material condition."

Although the church will not participate in medical
research, followers of Christian Science have been
studied to determine whether they live as long as those
who rely on orthodox medicine.
In 1989 Dr. William Franklin
Simpson reported in the Journal
of the American Medical
Association that graduates from
Principia College, a liberal arts
college for Christian Scientists,
"had a significantly higher death
rate than the control population"
who attended the University of
Kansas in Lawrence.

The church believed that the
study was "seriously marred by
misleading assumptions and
incomplete data." In the words of
Nathan A. Talbot, Manager of
Committees on Publication: "The
actual experiences of healing in Christian Scientists'
lives have simply been too substantial and meaningful
to be dismissed in the long run."

> While convalescing from
> severe injuries sustained in
> a fall, Eddy was reading her
> Bible. When she read about
> Jesus' raising of the palsied
> man, God's presence
> suddenly seemed to flood
> her being, and she too rose
> from her bed healed.

PAINLESS ECSTASY

Walking on fire without being burned, hanging with hooks through the flesh without bleeding, handling poisonous snakes without being bitten — some people in a state of religious trance or ecstasy seem impervious to pain or injury.

FIRE-WALKING WORKSHOP

Since 1987, Christina Thomas of Tennessee has been organizing fire walks around the U.S. The fire walkers build their own bonfire, using ordinary logs dowsed with kerosene. When the fire is lit, they stand in a circle and Thomas advises them to observe their feelings and confront their fears.

Thomas then plays a tape of the rhythmic, powerful sounds of a

A novice fire walker

mother's heartbeat as it might be heard by an unborn child. The fire walkers dance to the rhythm.

Hot, glowing coals

Blowing a conch shell and banging a drum, Thomas leads the way to the fire. She rakes it out into a bed of hot, glowing coals. Twenty minutes later, Thomas rolls her eyes upward and strolls across the 10-foot-long fire path. One by one the others follow, each giving a celebratory yell at the end.

Thomas compares the experience with riding a bike. "Once you learn, you can always remember how to find that balance. In the future, when you face an obstacle, you will remember the state of awareness that allowed you to walk unharmed through the burning coals, and that will help you to face the challenge."

ORDEAL BY FIRE HAS BEEN A FEATURE of many religious ceremonies throughout the world. Missionaries described in the 18th century how the American Indians of the St. Lawrence River and Great Lakes regions handled burning coals and walked through fire without ill-effect. In Hawaii, India, and elsewhere, observers can witness the same phenomenon today. Usually the ordeal is undertaken to purge sins.

Razor-sharp hooks

At religious festivals in India, penitents have razor-sharp hooks inserted in their flesh and are then hung in the air by ropes. They reportedly do not bleed, their flesh does not seem to tear, and they apparently show no sign of distress.

In the southern U.S. there are some religious sects that handle poisonous snakes and even drink poison. They take literally the words of the Bible: "They will pick up serpents, and if they drink any deadly thing, it will not hurt them." (Mark 16:18)

A scientific sole
German psychologist Dr. Wolfgang Larbig, of the University of Tübingen, wanted to see if changes in the body and brain inhibited the sensation of pain. In one experiment he reduced a fire to ashes at about 302°F (150°C). He then nailed a piece of pigskin on a wooden leg and "walked" it across. When the temperature of the foot was measured, it was much lower than that of the ashes. Despite the pigskin insulation, however, the heat could still scorch flesh.

A test of faith
A devotee braves the flames at a Hindu religious festival in Bombay.

Snakes alive!

The Jolo Serpent Handlers of the Church of the Lord Jesus Christ in the Appalachian Mountains prove their faith by handling dangerous snakes, such as rattlesnakes and copperheads, and drinking small amounts of strychnine (a poison that causes seizures) during their services. It has been suggested that few people are bitten because the snakes are rendered harmless by the hypnotic swaying and chanting of the congregation.

Self-mutilation

A devotee at the Thaipusam Festival procession, Singapore. Research has shown that fakirs and devotees who subject their bodies to such tortures without apparently feeling pain are in a different state of mind from normal consciousness. Their brain waves include theta rhythms, normally found only when the subject is in deep sleep.

The hanged man

This devotee is demonstrating his faith at the spring Muslim festival (*charokh puja*) near Srimangal, Bangladesh. The hooks are strategically placed so that the flesh does not tear, and bleeding is kept to a minimum by pinching the flesh before it is pierced.

Flemish flagellants

Self-flagellation has been practiced by religious fanatics for centuries. These flagellants, from Doornik in Belgium, were part of a mid-14th-century movement. It was a popular conception in Europe at that time that the Messiah would return to earth, and these flagellants were seeking to purge themselves of their sins before the Day of Judgment.

CASEBOOK
FAITH HEALING

Kathryn Kuhlman, one of the best-known faith healers of the 20th century, took no personal credit for her sometimes apparently miraculous "cures." She attributed them all to the power of the Holy Spirit.

O N OCTOBER 27, 1949, PAUL GUNN attended a religious service conducted by Kathryn Kuhlman in the auditorium of the Carnegie Library, Pittsburgh, Pennsylvania. He had advanced cancer of the left lung, walked with difficulty with the help of two canes, and was in great pain. He was booked into the city's Presbyterian Hospital for surgery two days later to remove the lung.

The power of God
He never needed the operation. He walked out of the service that night without his canes, upright and well. He describes what happened in his own words: "Suddenly the power of God came down. It hit me and just for an instant the sensation of burning fire in my lung was more intense than it had ever been before. I thought I couldn't stand it....And then, it was all over — just like that. You know how when you light a piece of paper, it all crumbles up into ashes. Well, my chest felt as if a match had been struck to a piece of paper inside it. And then it seemed as if God had just touched the pile of ashes, and they all fell away, and from that moment on there was no more burning, no more pain, no more ache. And there hasn't been, from that day to this."

No sign of cancer
Two days after the service, Gunn returned to the hospital. There he was thoroughly examined, and underwent a series of laboratory tests, including X-rays and a bronchoscopy. The test results apparently showed that no sign of the cancer remained. Within days, Gunn was back at work. Records show that he was at the same job 12 years later, and had not missed a single day due to illness since his cure.

Extract taken from *I Believe in Miracles* (1962) by Kathryn Kuhlman.

THE SKEPTICAL DOCTOR

Dr. William A. Nolen attended one of Kuhlman's services as an usher, and described the event:

"Every few minutes Kuhlman would pause, turn as if she had heard a voice, and point out into the audience. 'Back there,' she said on one occasion, 'way back on the right. There's a man with cancer in his hip. You're cured. Your pain is gone. Come and claim your cure.' Someone back in the hall struggled to his feet and slowly worked his way down the aisle. Behind him came one of the ushers, carrying his wheelchair. When he got closer I saw that he was the fellow I had talked to earlier, the man with cancer of the kidney.

Is that your wheelchair?

"When he was up on the stage Kathryn Kuhlman said, 'Is that your wheelchair?'

'Yes, it is,' said the man, bewildered.

'And now you're walking. Isn't that wonderful? Praise the Lord. What do you think of that?' Kathryn asked, turning to the audience. Enthusiastic applause.

'You've had cancer in the hip and now your pain is gone; is that right?' she asked.

'Yes,' he answered.

'Bend over so everyone can see.'

He bent over.

'Walk around.'

He walked around.

'Isn't the Holy Spirit wonderful!' she sighed, and another usher helped the man off the stage."

Migraines and varicose veins

Dr. Nolen followed up several of the "cures." He reported that some ailments such as migraines and varicose veins had been alleviated, but this was not surprising, since such ailments are liable to clear up at any time. None of the apparently miraculous cures turned out to be permanent.

The daughter of the man with cancer of the kidney said this about her father's health:

"After the service he felt real good for about three or four days. Then he began to get weak again and we took him back to the doctor. The doctor took X-rays and told us that the tumor had grown some more, and that was making Dad's blood drop. So he gave him a transfusion and changed his medicines around. Since then he's had to go back weekly for shots. He's losing weight and he needs pain pills now for his back.

"I guess Dad was wrong when he thought Kathryn Kuhlman had cured him."

Extract taken from *Healing: A Doctor in Search of a Miracle* (1974) by William A. Nolen, M.D

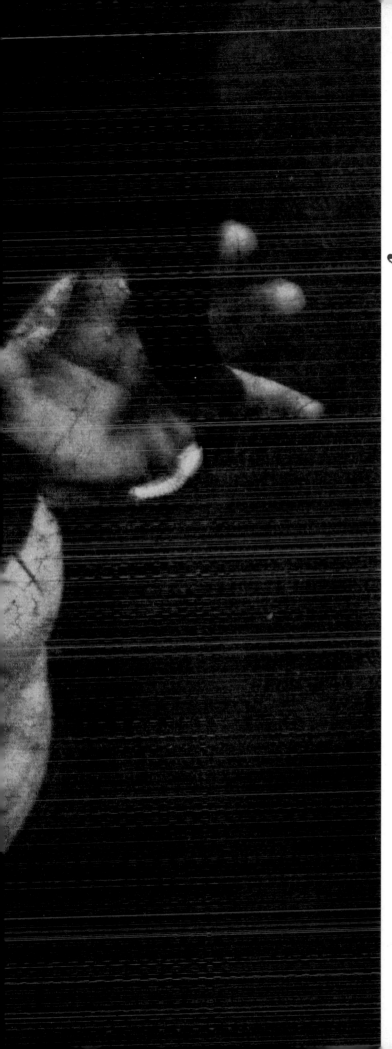

THE GUIDING SPIRIT

Some healers believe they function as mediums for a controlling spirit that guides their actions. Such psychic healers seem to have achieved remarkable results, but are their powers really paranormal?

ORN IN 1877, THE SON of a Kentucky farmer, Edgar Cayce was only seven or eight when he had his first mystic experience. According to his biography, *The Sleeping Prophet* (1967), by Jess Stearn, he was reading the Bible one day when he became aware of a bright figure asking him what request he would like granted.

"Just that I may be helpful to others," the boy replied, "especially to children who are ill."

Universal Consciousness

The next day thoughts of the vision prevented him from learning his spelling words. That night he heard a voice within him repeating, "Sleep, and we may be able to help you." When he awoke a few minutes later, he apparently knew by heart every word in his spelling book. This was how, he remembered, he first experienced the power that he called Universal Consciousness.

In his early twenties Cayce lost his voice. After fruitlessly seeking help from doctors, he met a hypnotist named Al Layne, who put him into a trance and told him to diagnose

Edgar Cayce

his own condition and cure himself. Cayce did so, and was surprised to find that his voice had returned.

The next day, again under hypnosis, Cayce diagnosed a chronic illness of Layne's that had baffled doctors, and prescribed treatment. The diagnosis was delivered in medical terminology that in his normal waking state was apparently meaningless to him.

Diagnosis from a distance

So began Cayce's remarkable career of psychic diagnosis and prescription. Preferring not to meet his patients, he simply took their name and address. He then put himself into a trance, gave a diagnosis (or a reading, as he called it), and recommended a type of treatment. Sometimes the medicines he suggested were obscure or old-fashioned, but they seemed to work.

In 1909 Dr. Wesley Ketchum, of Cayce's hometown, Hopkinsville, was so impressed by Cayce's diagnoses that he wrote to the American Society of Clinical Research in Boston. An article in *The New York Times* followed, and Cayce, to his professed alarm, became

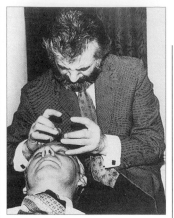

George Chapman

GUIDED "SURGERY"

A healer who claims to be completely controlled by his spirit guide is George Chapman, a former fireman, of Liverpool, England, who took up spiritualism in 1944 after the death of his infant daughter. Chapman says that the spirit who spoke to him during his deep trance states gave his name as Dr. William Lang. Chapman set about tracing Lang and discovered that in life he had been a celebrated eye specialist. He had died in 1937 at the age of 84.

"Spirit body"

In the trance state Chapman mimes surgery, under Lang's guidance, on fully conscious, fully dressed patients. He "operates" with imaginary surgical instruments on the "spirit body," a few inches above the physical body. While he does so he speaks in Lang's voice, using correct medical terminology. Witnesses who had known Lang were convinced that the voice really was the doctor's.

Future partnership

It seems that the Chapman-Lang partnership, if it exists at all, might well continue into the next generation. According to Dr. Robert W. Laidlaw of the American Society for Psychical Research, Lang told him, through Chapman, that after the latter's death, his son Michael will take over his work and be guided by Lang's son, the late Dr. Basil Lang.

famous. For the next 35 years he diagnosed on a full-time basis.

In 1931, at Virginia Beach, Cayce founded the Association for Research and Enlightenment to keep and maintain records of his thousands of cases. These are still studied by researchers for the insights they may provide on the diagnosis and treatment of illness.

Cayce also gave readings on clients' previous incarnations, prophesied future events, and published books about his ability to see into the past and the future. When he died in 1945, he had become known as one of the outstanding psychics of the century.

The "simpleton"

About 10 years after Cayce's death, another celebrated psychic launched his healing career in Brazil. This was José de Freitas, known locally as Arigó (meaning "simpleton" or "yokel"). Born in 1921, he was the son of a farmer, could barely read or write, and lived in the small town of Congonhas do Campo.

Arigó's guiding spirit was a dead German surgeon, Dr. Adolf Fritz, who appeared to him in dreams and hallucinations. Night after night, Arigó would awake sweating and trembling after dreaming of a plump, balding man who told him in guttural tones: "You will heal many." Whether Fritz was a real person is, however, doubtful — no supporting evidence for

> **The operations were carried out at lightning speed, using such implements as nail scissors and a rusty penknife, and with no resort to anesthetics.**

his existence has ever been found.

Despite an exorcism performed by a parish priest, the spirit continued his visits. One day, according to John G. Fuller in his biography of the healer, the spirit forced Arigó into action. A friend of the family was dying of cancer of the uterus. Arigó reportedly entered her room with a kitchen knife and plunged it into the woman's body. After twisting the knife violently, he supposedly felt in the wound and withdrew a tumor as big as a grapefruit. Then he began to sob. A local doctor was called, so the story goes, and he confirmed that the woman was cured.

Arigó's fame as a healer spread, and he became a national hero. He turned away no one who came to him for help, and he is estimated to have treated more than half a million patients.

Nail scissors and penknife

Dr. Andrija Puharich, a New York parapsychologist, believes he personally experienced Arigó's powers. He not only observed Arigó at first hand, but had a small lipoma (a type of benign tumor) painlessly removed from his forearm with a penknife. Dr. Ary Lex, a noted Brazilian surgeon, and lecturer at the São Paulo University Medical School, watched Arigó perform four operations. They were carried out at lightning speed, using such implements as nail scissors and a rusty penknife, and with no anesthetic. Lex was reportedly satisfied that he could detect no evidence of trickery.

Dr. William Lang

Arigó at work
José de Freitas (known as Arigó) conducting an eye operation under the spirit guidance of Dr. Adolf Fritz.

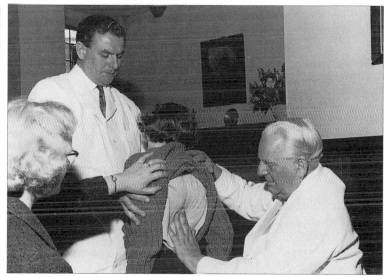

Healing hands
Spiritualist healer Harry Edwards at work on a patient in his Healing Sanctuary.

Arigó died in a car crash in 1971 at the age of 49. Despite criticisms leveled at him in the decades since, he remains one of the most convincing of all paranormal surgeons — and his methods are still a profound mystery.

Help from the great

It is only at a late stage in their career that some psychic healers realize that they may be under the guidance of a spirit. Such an alleged healer was an English spiritualist Harry Edwards. From the 1940's to the mid-1970's he helped thousands of people from his Healing Sanctuary in Surrey, England, and many more who attended his public healing demonstrations throughout Britain, Holland, South Africa, and Zimbabwe.

In his book *Thirty Years a Spiritual Healer* (1968), Edwards describes how he discovered his healing potential during the First World War, when he was in charge of a crew of Arabs laying railroads in the Middle East. The Arabs told him that when he treated the wounds and injuries they incurred at work, they healed faster than when others treated them. They began to call him *hakim,* meaning "healer."

Later in the war, Edwards encountered further evidence of his healing powers, but when peace came, he did not pursue his apparent gift. Then in 1935 he became interested in the Spiritualist Church, and soon after had his first experience with spiritual healing. A friend told him of a man who was dying of tuberculosis in a hospital. Edwards and his friend meditated, hoping for the man's recovery, and Edwards had a vivid vision of him, in the last bed but one in the ward. (He later discovered that the vision was correct.) The next day the man began to recover.

Edwards then started performing an ever-increasing number of apparently spiritual healings, most of which were in the form of "absent healing," organized by correspondence. He dealt with thousands of patients a week in this way.

Expert assistance

Edwards claimed that as his healing powers increased, he discovered that he was being assisted in his work by two great scientists of the past: the French pioneer in the field of bacteriology, Louis Pasteur, and the English champion of antisepsis, Joseph Lister.

Edwards, who died in 1976, described himself as a channel through whom spirit healing energies were transmitted. He claimed that over 85 percent of all those who came to him for spiritual healing received appreciable easement and benefit; and of that figure about 30 percent reported a full recovery.

Louis Pasteur
A 19th-century cartoon of Pasteur, allegedly one of the guiding spirits behind the healing work of Harry Edwards.

QUESTIONABLE REPUTATIONS

Although many people have been impressed by what they have seen of spirit-guided healers, others have been distinctly unimpressed. One such was the late Dr. William A. Nolen, surgeon and author, who from 1972 to 1974 investigated the claims of several such healers.

Avoiding responsibility

In his book, *Healing: A Doctor in Search of a Miracle* (1974), Dr. Nolen argued that all psychic healers have acquired their reputation on questionable grounds. First, when they are unable to heal, they excuse themselves by saying that their guiding spirit is not with them that day, or that the patient does not have enough faith. In this way, they take no personal responsibility for their failures.

Spontaneous remission

Second, the claim of spirit-guided healers to have on average a 70 percent cure rate means very little; roughly 80 percent of all illnesses, if left untreated, eventually clear up of their own accord.

Third, psychic healers' most impressive alleged successes are with stress-related illnesses such as asthma, migraine, and certain types of ulcer. Healers cannot, says Dr. Nolen, cure purely organic diseases such as infections, broken bones, and cancer. This, of course, is a claim that psychic surgeons and their patients would dispute.

PSYCHIC SURGERY

Perhaps the most dramatic form of all alleged psychic healing is the apparent removal of diseased tissue by surgery carried out with the bare hands. But is this possible — or is it all a skillful conjuring trick?

Hands-on surgery
Psychic surgeons are most common in the Philippines and in South America. Over the years their activities have been investigated by a number of scientific observers and laymen. The reports of these investigators have been inconclusive. Here Edivaldo da Silva, one of the best known of the many Brazilian practitioners, is shown at work.

*I*N SOME PARTS OF THE WORLD, people with no special medical knowledge or qualifications regularly perform "operations" that make no use of surgical instruments and yet seem to bring about amazing cures. In an operation of this highly controversial type, the patient remains fully clothed, with only the diseased area exposed, and is given no anesthetic. The psychic surgeon then appears to make an opening in the body with his bare hands. And the psychic incision seems to bleed in the way a normal surgical incision might. The surgeon then seems to plunge both hands into the opening and extract a tumor, cyst, or other portion of diseased tissue. After the blood is wiped away there is no sign of any wound.

Something very extraordinary?

In his book *The Romeo Error* (1976), the celebrated biologist and researcher Lyall Watson gives a detailed account of one of over a thousand Filipino psychic operations that he has witnessed. He was apparently convinced that this operation was a genuine demonstration of psychic surgery. Watson concluded with the statement: "Something very extraordinary still happens in the Philippines."

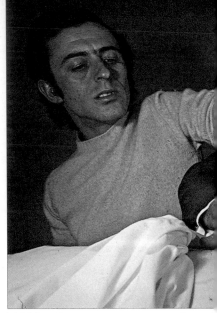

Faking it
One of a series of photographs produced by the Jesuit Father Quevedo to show how easy it is to fake psychic surgery. Father Quevedo is head of the Latin American Parapsychology Council. The Catholic Church is skeptical about the claims of the psychic surgeons, many of whom belong to the Spiritist Church.

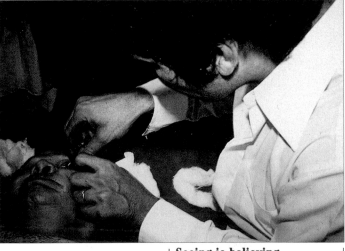

Seeing is believing
Psychic surgeons do not seem to flinch from operations on the most delicate and sensitive organs of the body. Ivan Trilha of Paraguay, for example, specialized in operations on the eye.

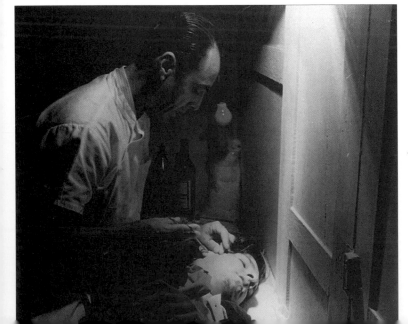

Brain surgery
Here Antonio Oliviera Sales, a psychic surgeon based in Brazil, appears to perform a delicate operation on the brain. Sales was a bricklayer before he began his healing career in the early 1950's.

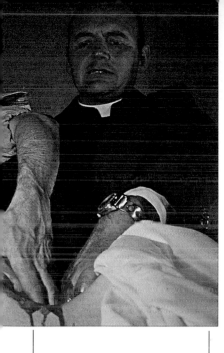

"Doctor Tony"

Filipino psychic surgeon Antonio "Doctor Tony" Agpaoa blows on his hands (below) before beginning an operation to remove a malignant growth in the uterus. In 1968 Agpaoa (pictured with his attorney, left) was arraigned on fraud charges in Detroit. Over a hundred Detroit patients had traveled to the Philippines and paid him for "bloodless operations." On return to the U.S., many of the patients said that they felt no better. In 1979 Agpaoa was admitted to a hospital with appendicitis — under an assumed name. He apparently preferred to resort to conventional surgery when his own body was involved. He was reported to have confided to the surgeon conducting the operation: "You know, doc, physicians can't heal themselves."

Screen exposé

In 1979 the BBC investigated the claims of husband-and-wife team David and Helen Elizalde to be able to perform successful psychic surgery. They filmed the Elizaldes at work, and asked psychic researcher and professional magician James Randi to comment on their performance. Randi was convinced that the Elizaldes were frauds. This view was reinforced when the research team managed to acquire some bloodstained material from an alleged psychic operation. Forensic scientists analyzed the blood and reported that it came from a pig.

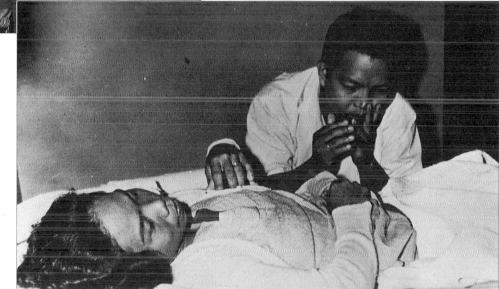

Tricks of the trade

Arch-skeptic and magician James Randi believes that psychic surgeons rely on simple sleight of hand and conjuring tricks to achieve their sometimes astonishing illusions of actual surgery. He claimed that psychic surgeons never actually open the bodies of their patients, and that the blood is produced by the surgeon "palming" and opening sachets of pig's blood.

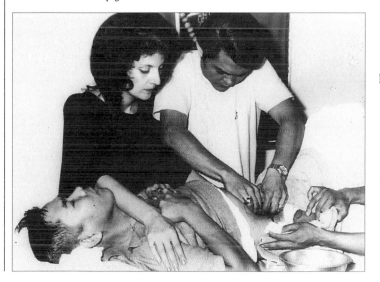

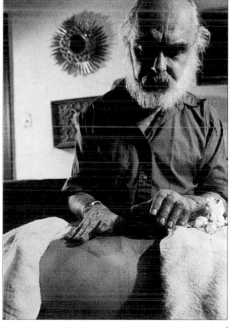

CHAPTER THREE

THE WISDOM OF THE EAST

The needle treatments of acupuncture, the balancing of yin and yang in the diet, the dance-like exercises of tai chi, the breathing techniques of yoga — all these Eastern practices have the same aim: maintaining within a person the life force responsible for physical health and spiritual well-being.

Michael walked up and down the room slowly, stooped over and still in great pain from his badly strained back. He looked down at his right hand. The acupuncturist had inserted two extremely fine needles in the back of it. His hand tingled slightly, but that was all. Suddenly he felt the pain in his back beginning to ease.

Earlier in the day Michael, a 48-year-old engineer, had tried to lift a heavy box of

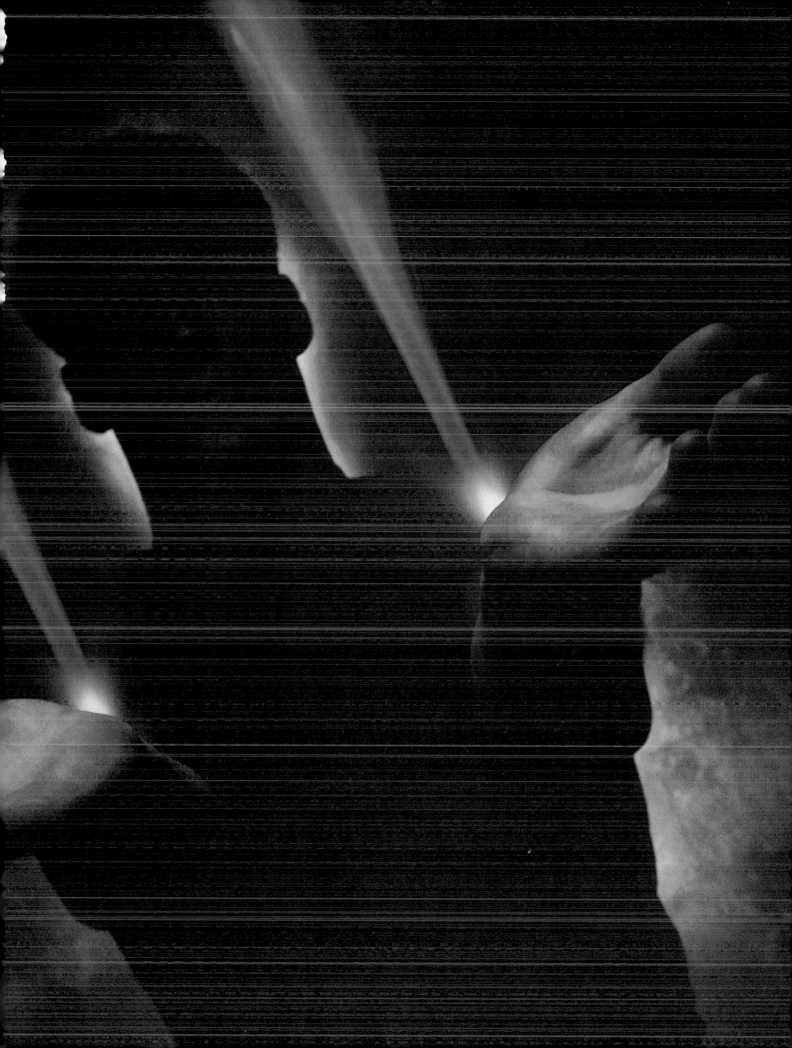

books; instantly, he was doubled over in pain and could barely move. Now, as the acupuncturist removed the needles 20 minutes after they had been inserted, the pain was almost gone and he was able to stand upright. The acupuncturist told Michael that he would have to rest to allow the injury to heal and would need further treatment the next day — but that the initial treatment had worked because it had cleared the blocked energy in his back.

Life force

In the West the use of acupuncture is not widespread. In China, however, acupuncture accounts for 20 percent of all medical treatment. Every day thousands of patients are successfully treated by this technique, as patients have been for over 2,000 years.

How does acupuncture work? The Chinese explain it in the following way. Central to the treatment, and to other forms of traditional Chinese medicine, is the idea of *qi* (pronounced "chee"), a life force, or vital energy, within the body. This concept is common to many Eastern cultures and in the West is generally called *chi*. An adequate amount of chi is considered to be absolutely essential for good health: without enough, a person may become listless, weak, and unable to remain warm. Just as important is the flow of chi: if it is blocked, for example, the result can be depression, irritability, or, as in Michael's case, pain.

The Chinese believe that chi is produced and stored by each organ inside the human body. Connecting the organs with each other, and with the head, arms, and legs, is a system of 12

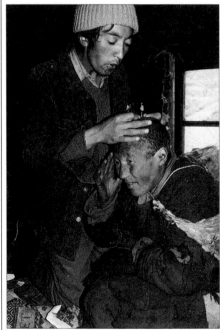

Welcome relief
A Tibetan doctor, working in Tarr village in the Ladakh region of Kashmir, India, uses moxibustion to treat a nun suffering from severe migraine.

invisible pathways running through the body. Chi flows along these pathways, also known as meridians.

Each meridian is named after the organ or function with which it is particularly associated — for example, there is a heart meridian and a kidney meridian. The acupuncture needle points lie along these meridians. There are almost 1,000, but only about a third are used by acupuncturists.

Burning points

Some acupuncturists warm the acupuncture point by using a technique known as moxibustion. Moxibustion refers to the burning of the downy covering of the leaves of the herb *Artemisia moxa*. The acupuncture needle is heated from above by burning the herb over it. However, moxibustion is sometimes applied without the use of needles at all. A small cone of the moxa is ignited near the chosen acupuncture

> Connecting the organs with each other, and with the head, arms, and legs, is a system of 12 invisible pathways running through the body. Chi flows along these pathways, also known as meridians.

Power lines
This model shows the position of the body's 12 pathways, or, meridians, along which the vital life force, chi, is thought to flow.

A BALANCED DIET

The Oriental idea of healthy diet differs fundamentally from the Western. In the Far East the "heating" or "cooling" properties of foods are considered to be as significant as their vitamin content and to be an important factor in creating and maintaining inner harmony.

*I*N THE MAINTENANCE OF GOOD HEALTH, diet has long been allocated a much more important role by the East than by the West. And Oriental ideas about what constitutes a good diet are markedly different from Western ideas, going far beyond such concepts as vitamins, proteins, and carbohydrates. They are based on two opposing principles, yin and yang, which lie at the heart of ancient Chinese thought. Yin represents the soft, quiet, slow, dark female extreme. Yang is the hard, active, quick, bright male extreme.

"Hot" and "cold" foods

Applied to diet, yin is used to describe "cold" food, yang "hot." These terms do not refer to the temperature of the food or necessarily to its degree of spiciness; they are used to describe the cooling or heating effect the food is considered to have on the body. Thus a yin food fresh from the oven will still be considered to be "cold" and refrigerated yang food still be "hot."

Yin foods include vegetables and fruit. It is thought that when eaten in excess they may cause chills, pallor,

> **Bad-tempered people with high coloring who eat meat and spicy foods may well be able to change themselves for the better by cutting down on their normal diet and eating more fruits and vegetables.**

moist coughs, low energy, and delayed recovery from illness. Yang foods include not only very spicy foods such as chilies and ginger but also coffee, alcohol (excluding beer), and meat. Among the heating effects they might produce are thirst, dry throat, sweating, flushed face, and cracks at the corners of the mouth.

Providing the right balance

Foods somewhere in the middle of the yin-yang spectrum, considered to be neither particularly cooling nor heating, include fish, eggs, grains, and dates. Acid- and alkaline-forming foods do not correlate exactly with yin and yang foods, but foods mainly from the center of the yin-yang scale are generally mildly acid- or alkaline-forming. Foods in the middle range can help to

> **A balanced diet produces harmony throughout the body and helps maintain a free flow of vital energy.**

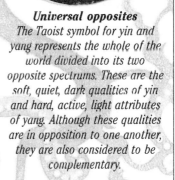

Universal opposites
The Taoist symbol for yin and yang represents the whole of the world divided into its two opposite spectrums. These are the soft, quiet, dark qualities of yin and hard, active, light attributes of yang. Although these qualities are in opposition to one another, they are also considered to be complementary.

provide the right dietary balance, but an overconsumption of them is considered to be as potentially harmful as an excess of hot or cold foods.

The Chinese believe a good diet to be one that includes a variety of foods that balance yin and yang. It is also important not to consume too much food of one particular taste (sour, bitter, sweet, pungent, or salty). Such a balanced diet produces harmony throughout the entire body and helps maintain a free flow of vital energy. A person in this condition is able to respond to physical and emotional influences from outside without becoming overly stressed or ill.

Seen in this way, diet may be used to correct imbalances in the person, devotees maintain. Bad-tempered people with high coloring who eat meat and spicy foods may well be able to change themselves for the better by cutting down on their normal diet and eating more fruits and vegetables. Dreamy people with low energy, on the other hand, followers say, may benefit from eating more meat or spicy foods such as chili peppers or hot sauces.

Personalized diet

In this system of thought there is no single "best" diet for any person all of the time. Instead it is believed that we all should be constantly aware of variations in our bodies and feelings so that we can make the necessary changes in what we eat.

NEW LIFE

Penny, a 29-year-old social worker, had suffered from bronchitis for years as the result of smoking. She decided to try acupuncture to help her quit the habit.

The acupuncturist explained that habitual smoking congests the lungs and that this blocks the flow of chi (vital energy) in them. Since the lungs help chi circulate throughout the body, this blockage affects overall health. It was responsible for the chronic eczema and crippling menstrual pains that also plagued Penny. Acupuncture would not only enable Penny to stop smoking but also would help restore her normal lung function and improve her other problems.

Dramatic improvement

After her fourth session of treatment, Penny had stopped smoking completely, her bronchitis had eased, her eczema had cleared up considerably, and she had an almost pain-free period for the first time in her life. Continued treatment produced further improvement. For Penny acupuncture had brought about an amazing change in the quality of her life.

point. Alternatively, the moxa is rolled into a stick and the lighted end of the stick is held close to the skin at the appropriate point.

Yin and yang

In order to make a diagnosis, the acupuncturist first asks the patient about his or her illness, general health, and medical history. Patients are also asked about their diet, exercise, sex life, and general lifestyle. It is believed that poor nutrition or excessive sexual activity, for example, can be harmful to chi generally. And stress is thought to disturb in particular the chi of some major internal organs, such as the heart and liver.

In addition, the acupuncturist studies the condition of the tongue and feels the six pulse points in each wrist (one for each meridian). All this information is used as a guide to the flow of chi in the body and the balance in it of yin and yang, the two opposing principles that lie

> **Having determined which meridian is functioning abnormally, the acupuncturist inserts needles (generally between two and eight in number) into the skin at points along that meridian.**

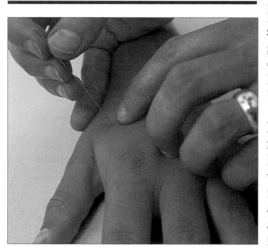

Specific point
An acupuncturist inserts a needle into a point on the large intestine meridian on a patient's left hand.

at the heart of traditional Chinese thought. Yin is cold, wet, and passive, yang warm, dry, and active. Certain organs, meridians, foods, climatic conditions, and other influences are said to be yin, others yang. The Chinese believe that over-dominance of one or the other principle in a person causes sickness and that good health depends on a harmonious balance of the two.

Inserting the needles

Having determined which meridian is functioning abnormally, the acupuncturist inserts needles (generally between two and eight in number) into the skin at points along that meridian. This is either to stimulate or to reduce circulation of chi. Needles used today are of stainless steel, not much thicker than a human hair, solid not hollow, and about 1–1½ inches long. The needles are usually inserted to a depth of about ¼–1¼ inches, vertically, obliquely, or horizontally. Often the acupuncturist rotates them, either throughout the treatment or at certain specific intervals of time.

Each acupuncture point produces an effect on a specific part of the body, practitioners claim. Some may have a local effect, while others may act on a distant part. Michael's treatment was of the latter type. The needles in his hand stimulated the flow of chi in a meridian that ran over the injured part of his back. This is what relieved his pain, his acupuncturist told him, and set him on the road to recovery.

Acupuncture needles

On the left is a traditional Chinese needle, with a filigree handle. Next to it is a "hair" needle with its guiding tube, which is used for accurate work on delicate areas of the body. To its right are three modern disposable needles, followed by gold, silver, and steel needles. The plastic device contains a small needle, which is left in place in the ear for the treatment of addictive behavior, such as smoking or alcoholism.

THE MYSTERY OF THE PAINLESS NEEDLES

Extensive scientific research into how the acupuncture technique works has been carried out in the West. Despite rigorous testing, however, the investigators have failed to come up with any clear-cut answers.

THE PAIN RELIEF PRODUCED by acupuncture has been the area most investigated by Western researchers. One explanation, the "gate" theory, is that the acupuncture needle stimulates nerve fibers that "close the gate on" the transmission of pain from its localized site up to the brain. This does not, however, fully explain why the pain relief achieved by acupuncture has been known to last for many months.

Another theory is that acupuncture stimulates the release into the central nervous system of endorphins, a group of natural painkilling substances produced in the brain: these substances normally take about 20 minutes to relieve pain. Acupuncture needling, however, sometimes produces instant relief.

Animal magic
Skeptics cannot explain why acupuncture seems to work on animals, which should presumably be immune to the power of suggestion.

Success with animals

A further hypothetical explanation for the reported success of acupuncture in pain relief is that it is no more than a form of hypnosis. However, this suggestion is not borne out by findings that show that it works as well on those who are not

> "In more than 600 cases of coronary heart disease, the effectiveness of acupuncture in relieving the symptoms was over 80 percent."
> *World Health*, **the magazine of the World Health Organization**

suggestible as on those who are. Moreover, it is also effective on animals, who do not appear to be susceptible to hypnosis. For example, Dr. John Nicol, a veterinarian practicing in Guildford, England, has used acupuncture with repeated success to treat lameness in horses.

In addition, these theories do not explain acupuncture's success with nonpainful illnesses such as certain infectious diseases. For example, the December 1979 edition of *World Health*, the magazine of the World Health Organization, contained the following data regarding treatment of disease by acupuncture: "In 645 cases of acute bacillary dysentery 90 percent of the patients were cured within 10 days as judged by clinical symptoms and signs." And "In more than 600 cases of coronary heart disease, the effectiveness of acupuncture in relieving the symptoms was over 80 percent."

Whether or not medical science ever comes up with a completely satisfactory answer to the mystery of the mechanisms behind acupuncture, many Western doctors no longer dispute that it works to relieve pain.

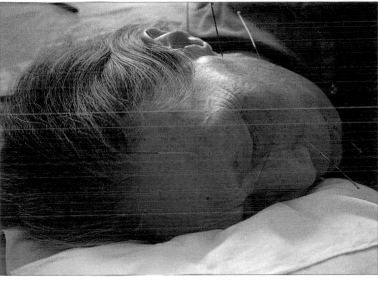

Out cold
This patient undergoing treatment at a Shanghai hospital benefits from the use of acupuncture as an anesthetic prior to an operation.

MEDITATION IN MOTION

Resembling a dance in slow motion, tai chi is an ancient Chinese system of gentle, flowing exercises. Performed well, they produce a feeling of relaxation and are claimed to keep the mind and body healthy.

A GROUP OF AMERICANS, under the instruction of a Chinese teacher, is practicing a flowing pattern of bodily movements. Balancing the weight on the right foot, each person gently swings the right hand up in front of the head. Then the right knee bends, the right hand slowly falls, and the trunk rotates easily to the right. The group is practicing White Crane Spreads Wings, one of the movements of tai chi chuan, a system of ancient Chinese exercises, generally known by the shortened form tai chi (pronounced "tie chee"). The object of these exercises, whose origins go back to about 2000 B.C., is to facilitate the free flow through the body of chi, the life force. This induces relaxation and, it is believed, builds up energy and ensures good health.

Practiced by millions in China, tai chi was largely unknown elsewhere until the mid-19th century.

Heavenly movement
A group of people practicing tai chi exercises outside the Temple of Heaven, Beijing.

Weight distribution

There are various styles of tai chi. The most popular in the West is Yang, named after a 19th-century practitioner Yang Lu-ch'an. The longer form of this style has more than 100 movements and takes up to 25 minutes to perform. The shorter form has 37 movements and takes up to 10 minutes. The movements are circular and consist chiefly of taking steps forward or backward, transferring weight from one leg to the other, rotating the trunk, and moving the hands and feet. They are performed gently and slowly, in combination with deep, even, abdominal breathing. Their basis is an

Serenity at dawn
A student meditates in the early morning on campus at the University of Beijing.

Fairy Weaving at the Shuttle, a tai chi movement

alternation of quiescence and activity: the body now yields, now advances, the hand now falls, now rises.

Many of the movements have names based on the natural world, the imagination, and daily life: Snake Creeps Down to the Water, Embrace the Tiger to Return to the Mountain, Fairy Weaving at the Shuttle, Needle at Sea Bottom.

Floating sensation

Most tai chi exercises are practiced to achieve relaxation and a feeling of well-being. The movements resemble a dance in slow motion — graceful and flowing — but the important process is actually occurring internally and cannot be seen: heart rate and breathing slow down, the nervous system becomes calmer. This state is sometimes described as a "meditation in motion" and often, believers claim, produces a sensation that is similar to floating.

The balanced art of tai chi

Some exercises, however, are used to practice self-defense. Practitioners are able to generate tremendous power at

---

Most tai chi exercises are practiced to achieve relaxation and a feeling of well-being.

---

will. But such power can also be used for therapeutic purposes. The energy is usually transmitted through the palm and, it is claimed, can be directed and focused at a diseased area.

Serious treatment

The Chinese believe that prolonged practice of tai chi improves the condition of the blood, bones, and internal organs and has mental and spiritual benefits. For this reason the large numbers who practice it mainly do so to achieve integration of mind and

body and to prevent disease. But it is also used as an actual treatment for many serious disorders, including some forms of cancer and heart disease. It is claimed that over 70 percent of sufferers treated in this way are subsequently able to lead relatively normal lives.

Currently, it is fashionable in the West to aim for a muscular, fit body. In the East the strenuous physical activity and competitiveness this involves are regarded as tension-making. There, in fact, the health of the internal body is seen as being of far greater importance than its external appearance.

Tai chi exercises require many years of practice, and even most of those who devote a lifetime to them never master them completely. For those, however, intent on reducing stress, it is claimed that tai chi can produce beneficial effects quite quickly. As tai chi exponent Stephen Annett says in *The Many Ways of Being* (1976), tai chi "is about finding the center of balance, with the physical center gradually leading to the spiritual center. It teaches the individual containment."

Embrace the Tiger to Return to the Mountain
Tai chi movements are meant to be performed with a relaxed mind and body. Performed well, the exercises should produce a floating sensation.

抱虎歸山

The ultimate aim of yoga, a Hindu system of philosophy, is to enable the practitioner, or yogi, to arrive at a state of inner harmony and to become united with the Universal Spirit, or Supreme Being.

Ancient postures
Hindu mythological figures are seen in various yogic postures on the facade of the Kapaleeshwara temple, Madras, India.

DEMANDING JOURNEY

By committing themselves to the demanding mental and physical discipline of yoga, practitioners hope not merely to improve their general health and fitness but, more profoundly, to travel the path to true enlightenment.

IN 1960, AT THE ALL-INDIA INSTITUTE of Medical Sciences, New Delhi, 36-year-old Sri Ramanand Yogi from Hyderabad was sealed in an airtight metal and glass box 6 x 4 x 4 feet. Despite the minimal amount of air in the box, he remained in it, fully conscious and without distress for 10 hours. Bal Krishnan Anand, a council member of the International Brain Research Organization and a member of the research team at the institute, found that the yogi had survived by reducing oxygen consumption and carbon dioxide elimination to a very low level. He had exerted tremendous conscious control over bodily processes that are normally not under conscious control.

Sri Ramanand Yogi's feat is an extreme — though far from exceptional — example of the self-mastery that an experienced yogi can achieve. But even ordinary practitioners of the discipline can attain some more modest degree of such power.

Inner harmony

The ultimate aim of yoga, a Hindu system of philosophy, is to enable the practitioner, or yogi, to arrive at a state of inner harmony and to become united with the Universal Spirit, or Supreme Being. In order to achieve this, the yogi must eliminate, by means of meditation and other techniques, such as fasting, all inner obstacles and impurities that prevent true self-knowledge. He or she must also develop his or her physical, spiritual, mental, and emotional potential to its full.

Images of men in yoga postures have been found on relics dating back to 2000 B.C. and before. And references to yoga are found in the Vedas, the earliest Hindu scriptures, first written about 1500–1200 B.C. Originally the principles and practices of yoga were handed down orally from gurus (spiritual teachers) to *chelas* ("disciples"). But around 300 B.C. these teachings were written down by Patañjali in his *yoga Sutra* (yoga Aphorisms), to make them available to everyone.

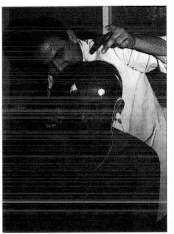

Under observation
Sri Ramanand Yogi prepares to reenact the experiment that he originally participated in 10 years before. For the second experiment, which took place on March 4, 1970, and was recorded on film, the yogi survived in an airtight container for just under six hours.

THE FASTING SAINT

One yogini (female yogi), Giri Bala, from northern Bengal, is claimed to have lived most of her life as a miracle: from girlhood the Fasting Saint, as she was known, lived without food or drink. In his *Autobiography of a Yogi* (1950), Swami Paramhansa Yogananda tells of his meetings with Giri Bala, who was then 68 years old. She told him how her guru initiated her into a *kriya* (cleansing technique) "that frees the body from dependence on the gross food of mortals....No medicine or magic is involved."

Maharaja's tests

Bala claimed that 25 years earlier she had agreed to have her fasting verified by tests monitored by the maharaja of Burdwan. She fasted for two months, locked away in the maharaja's palace, and later returned for two further periods of fasting of 20 and 15 days. According to Swami Paramhansa Yogananda, "these three rigorous scrutinies convinced him [the maharaja] beyond doubt" that Bala did not eat and was able to survive without food or drink.

▶ PAGE 77

ELEMENTAL HEALING

It is a Hindu belief that every person is made up of varying amounts of air, water, fire, earth, and ether. In Ayurveda, traditional Indian medicine, illness is thought to result from a disruption in the balance of these elements and can be cured only by restoring the balance.

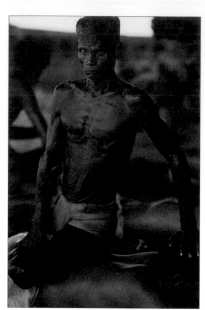

Under pressure
In Ayurvedic treatment, massage is used along with careful regulation of diet.

AYURVEDA (SCIENCE OF LIFE) is one of the most ancient and comprehensive of all medical systems. A treatise on it forms a section of the Vedas, the sacred Hindu texts written from about 1500 B.C. onward. Today Ayurveda is still practiced widely in India, Pakistan, and elsewhere in East Asia.

Hindu beliefs are founded on five elements of creation: air, water, fire, earth, and ether. These elements are manifested in human beings as three *doshas* (essences): *vata* (motion), a predominance of air and ether; *pitta* (energy), a predominance of fire; and *kapha* (inertia), a predominance of water and earth. Every individual is characterized by one of these *doshas* or, more commonly, by a particular combination of these five elements.

Medical market
An Ayurvedic practitioner displays his extensive wares at Anjuna market in Goa, India.

In their purest forms the three types are marked by the following characteristics. The *vata* type is thin, active, and quick-minded, but can easily become tired and anxious. The *pitta* type perspires a lot and has an oily skin, is ambitious and intelligent, but tends to be vain, intolerant, and aggressive. The *kapha* type is well built, but with a tendency to become overweight, is kind, tolerant, and loyal, but can be greedy and possessive.

By carefully observing and examining the patient, an Ayurvedic doctor can determine his or her character make-up and which elements have become out of balance. The pulse is examined and is characterized as "fast like the hopping of a frog" or "zigzagging like a snake." Also taken into account are, among other factors, the condition of the tongue, eyes, urine and feces; response to touch; age and lifestyle; the season; and how long the patient has been ill.

Treatment usually consists of a combination of any of the following: change of diet, medications, massage, breathing techniques, and exercises. Surgery will be performed if necessary.

In dietary treatment, taste is considered to affect different character types in different ways. Food with a pungent or bitter taste, for example, is considered the best kind for correcting an imbalance in a *kapha* person. In a *vata* person, however, such food may lead to muscle stiffness, insomnia, or constipation.

Feather ash

Over 8,000 different Ayurvedic medicines are described in the classic texts. They come mainly from plants. The ground root of turmeric, for example, is used in milk to treat bronchitis. Some medications are animal or mineral in origin, such as the ash of a peacock feather used to treat hiccups.

In Ayurvedic medicine no medication is ever regarded as an unqualified cure. Even when well, a person is expected to heed the doctor's counsel as to the quantity and quality of sleep, exercise, and food needed for good health. Ayurvedic medicine aims to prevent disease as well as to treat it.

The most celebrated section of the *yoga Sutra* is that dealing with the Eight Limbs. These are the eight stages of the yogic spiritual journey, whose ultimate aim is total liberation from the earthbound self. The stages are as follows. *Yama* is abstention from evil conduct, such as falsehood, violence, and theft. *Niyama* includes disciplines such as cleanliness, simplicity, and moderation. *Asana* are meditative postures. *Pranayama* is rhythmic and controlled breathing. *Pratyahara* is withdrawal of the mind from the world of the senses. *Dharana* is concentration. *Dhyana* is meditation. *Samadhi* is the final stage, a state in which the meditating self fuses with the object, or idea, of meditation. This leads to the merging of the self with the Universal Spirit.

Miraculous powers

According to the *yoga Sutra*, attaining the last three stages can give the yogi miraculous powers: the power to seem invisible, to see "beings of other dimensions," to levitate (float in the air), to understand the language of all creatures, to have insight into former incarnations, and to "penetrate the body and mind of another." These powers can be used to strengthen the practitioner's faith, but he or she must not look at them as an end in themselves. Dwelling on them becomes an obstacle to the achievement of *samadhi*.

These miraculous powers are said to be the mark of a true *siddha* ("sage" or "prophet"). There are documented cases of *siddhas* who apparently never show signs of aging. Some have lived for hundreds of years, followers claim.

Many paths

The various types of yogic discipline are known as paths. There are many different ones to choose from. Among the more important are the following.

Karma yoga, the path of action, teaches selfless service. It decrees that all of a person's actions are significant; and because yoga is founded on a belief in reincarnation, that they are significant not simply in this lifetime but in the next.

Therefore problems that we have to resolve in one lifetime may be the result of actions performed in a previous one. A karma yogi must work hard, casting aside all thought of praise or reward, whether in this life or the next.

Complete control

Raja yoga, the path of self-mastery, is for the individual who wishes to achieve complete control over his or her mind, senses, and emotions. The levels of concentration and meditation required by raja yoga cannot be attained until the body is functioning so perfectly that it offers no distractions to the self. To acquire such control over the body, it is

> There are documented cases of *siddhas* who apparently never show signs of aging.

necessary to practice the physical *asanas* of hatha yoga, a branch of raja yoga.

Before advanced hatha yoga can be performed, the yogi must carry out self-purification techniques called *kriyas*, to cleanse both the body and the mind. One *kriya* consists of washing out the large intestine by drawing water through it and then expelling the water. Another *kriya*, to clear the mind, involves staring unblinkingly at some object, such as a candle flame, until tears come.

Tantric yoga teaches that prosperity, fulfillment of sensual desires, spiritual and moral duty, and "release from it all" are all one. There are two paths of tantric yoga. One of these is especially spiritually challenging because it advocates that devotees indulge their desires to the point where these desires are exhausted and will eventually disappear. But followers of the more ascetic paths of yoga question this approach: they maintain that the

HEALTH BENEFITS

It is only during this century that the power of yoga has come to be appreciated in the West. Interest in meditation and particularly in the practice of hatha yoga postures grew after British army doctors in India sent home eyewitness reports of amazing yogic feats. And eventually the medical world at large began to take notice of the claimed benefits of the discipline. As reported in the magazine *Scientific American* in 1972, extensive research was carried out at Harvard Medical School on meditation and yoga methods of relaxation. It concluded that the techniques could benefit regular practitioners by reducing the effects of stress on their bodies.

Heart of the matter

In California, medical research has been carried out into the effects of lifestyle on heart disease. As reported in *The Lancet* (a British medical magazine) in 1990, the research indicated that yoga, in combination with dieting and aerobic exercises, is capable of reversing coronary heart disease.

Source of relief

In Britain, research by the Yoga Biomedical Trust has led to claims that yoga can relieve back pain, rheumatism, osteoarthritis, migraine, bronchitis, late-onset diabetes, asthma, and other disorders.

Yoga position
Parsvottanasana, *or The Flank*

HEALING PRESSURE

By exerting a controlled pressure on certain points of the feet or hands, practitioners of a form of therapy called reflexology claim to be able to relieve symptoms in other, unrelated, parts of the body.

REFLEXOLOGY HAS EVOLVED from an ancient form of pressure therapy known to many civilizations, including the Egyptian, as early as 3000 B.C. But no modern advances in the understanding and practice of it were made until the researches of Dr. William Fitzgerald, an American physician and surgeon, in the early 1900's.

Dr. Fitzgerald noted that when pressure was applied to the hands and feet of his patients, it noticeably lessened their pain during surgery. He investigated this phenomenon and discovered that for the purposes of his applied-pressure technique, he could divide the body into 10 longitudinal zones, five on each side of the spine. When he applied pressure to a zone, it appeared to have a reflex effect on the rest of that zone, relieving pain in any part of it.

Each of Dr. Fitzgerald's zones runs between a toe at one end and a finger or thumb at the other, passing en route through a leg, the torso, the head, and then an arm. For example, Zone 1 on the right side passed through various organs in the right central torso, through the right central part of the brain, and down the inner right arm to the thumb.

Energy channels

Dr. Fitzgerald regarded each zone as being rather like a meridian in acupuncture — an energy channel that can become blocked, leading to pain or dysfunction in any part of the zone. Since all the zones begin or end in the feet and hands, these were the areas Dr. Fitzgerald concentrated on for treatment. The idea was taken up by other doctors and came to be known as zone therapy.

In the 1930's Eunice D. Ingham, an assistant to Dr. Fitzgerald, continued his work of mapping which reflex points on the feet are linked to other parts of the body. She chose the feet rather than the hands because, being more sensitive, they are more responsive to this therapy. From her work, she developed the Ingham Method of Reflexology. Ingham's two books, *Stories the Feet Can Tell Thru Reflexology* (1938), and *Stories the Feet Have Told Thru Reflexology* (1951), became classic textbooks, and the therapy grew in popularity.

At the start of treatment, the reflexologist examines the reflex points on the patient's feet. These points are mostly on the sole, but some are on the upper part of the foot or a little way up the back of the leg. The reflexologist is searching for minute, sometimes grainy, crystalline deposits, which show up as tender areas. It is thought that these crystalline deposits are formed of metabolic waste under the skin. These indicate a blockage of energy in the relevant zone, a blockage that the patient is feeling as a pain or other discomfort elsewhere in the zone.

Wherever the reflexologist finds a crystalline deposit, he or she exerts pressure on it, using a specific form of reflex therapy massage. It is claimed that this disperses

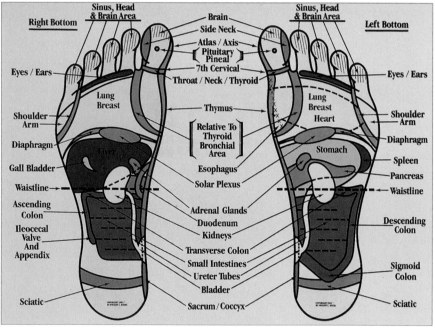

The original Ingham method
The official foot chart of the International Institute of Reflexology, which is based in St. Petersburg, Florida.

the crystals, and corrects the imbalance in zonal energy flow, and so helps to restore the patient to health.

Reflexology, its supporters claim, seems to be successful in easing pain. And practitioners claim that it can also be used to prevent the onset of many disorders. Eunice Ingham's own list of these is surprisingly wide-ranging and includes asthma, kidney disease, epilepsy, and arthritis.

As with the use of acupuncture as a method of healing, medical science currently has very little acceptance of reflexology and its effectiveness, and no convincing explanation of how it might work.

more one gives in to desires the more one becomes enslaved by them.

Other types of yoga include gnana yoga, the path of wisdom and knowledge, and bhakti yoga, the path of faith, love, and devotion. In the last hundred years or so, various yoga masters have come to the attention of the West. One of the first was Sri Paramhansa Ramakrishna (1836–86), who identified with the saints of many religions. At one time he even bore the stigmata of Christ on his hands. His leading disciple, Swami Vivekananda (1862–1902), attended the World Parliament of Religions in Chicago in 1893. Later he attracted huge audiences on his tour of the U.S.A. and Britain, when he claimed that all religions were only different paths to the one truth.

Another yogi who made an impact in the U.S.A. was Swami Paramhansa Yogananda (1893–1952), who left India in 1922 and sailed to California. There he founded the Self-Realization Fellowship. In 1952 he told his followers that his job on earth was done and he entered *mahasamadhi*, a yogi's final conscious exit from the body. Three weeks later a mortuary director recorded that his body showed no signs of decay. His life was full of apparently miraculous happenings, many of which are recorded in his *Autobiography of a Yogi*, published in 1950.

Performer of miracles

Sri Satya Sai Baba (born in 1926) has an ashram (religious retreat) near Bangalore. According to his many devotees, this yogi regularly performed miracles. Erlendur Haraldsson, professor of psychology at the University of Iceland, has described many of them in

Vivekananda claimed that all true religions were only different paths to the one truth.

Cause for celebration
The anniversary of Swami Vivekananda's birth is celebrated in West Bengal.

his book *Miracles Are My Visiting Cards*, published in 1987. They reportedly include sudden disappearances and reappearances before the eyes of his devotees, and producing objects out of nowhere. Sai Baba's message is that everyone must realize his or her divinity: "You are all God only you do not know it."

Promiscuity

One of the most controversial of all yoga masters was Bhagwan Shree Rajneesh (1931–89), who in 1981 established the city of Rajneeshpuram in Oregon. For stressed, repressed Westerners, Rajneesh devised a system of yoga called dynamic meditation. This involved breathing "chaotically," shouting mantras (words chanted during meditation), laughing, screaming, dancing, singing, and ultimately exhaustion. By 1970 the orange-clad followers of Rajneesh were wearing his image in a locket and had named him Bhagwan ("God" or "Supreme Lord").

Rajneesh advocated promiscuity as a means to transcendence. This made him very unpopular with the parents of his young followers. In 1985 various members of his organization were convicted of a number of crimes, including attempted murder. And in the same year Rajneesh himself was found guilty of arranging and performing sham marriages and other crimes. He was deported.

Famous disciples
Maharishi Mahesh Yogi with a group of followers, among them John Lennon and George Harrison of the Beatles.

GURU TO THE FAMOUS

"Twice a day for 15 minutes, stop your activity, close your eyes, and fathom the unboundedness deep within the mind to realize that fullness of life, that wholeness of life, that level of enlightenment which is kindled deep within everyone's heart." These are the words of Maharishi Mahesh Yogi (born in 1911), who developed the celebrated technique of transcendental meditation (TM) and in so doing made a discipline hitherto mysterious in the West available to everyone.

American success

The maharishi became fashionable and famous when in 1967 the Beatles visited his ashram (religious retreat) in India to study TM. He then toured the U.S.A. and Britain with other rock stars to promote his technique. At the height of TM's popularity, in the mid-1970's, some 50,000 Americans were attending courses at centers all around the country.

In 1971 the maharishi founded his own university, now situated in Fairfield, Ohio. This teaches psychology, neuroscience, and other academic subjects, and currently receives government research grants of several million dollars a year.

WHEELS OF ENERGY

Yogis and Buddhists believe that our well-being depends on energy fields within us that are far more subtle than the purely physical. Of major importance are the chakras — spinning centers of etheric energy — which distribute the force throughout our entire being.

> The etheric energy field consists of a network of energy lines — *nadis* — and, where the lines intersect, spinning energy centers — *chakras.*

*Y*OGIS AND BUDDHISTS HOLD THAT all human beings radiate an invisible, physical energy field. They also believe that overlapping this energy field is another more rarefied, known as the etheric energy field, which is itself overlapped by others yet more subtle. The etheric energy field consists of a network of energy lines — *nadis* — and, where the lines intersect, spinning energy centers — *chakras* (Sanskrit for wheels).

Energy controls

The chakras are said to take in, via food, air, and sunlight, the universal vital energy on which all life depends. They then distribute it, along the nadis, throughout the whole being.

In Indian tradition there are seven major chakras, situated at different points on the spine, each spinning at its own rate. The lower chakras spin more slowly than the upper ones. The seven are, in ascending order, the *muladhara* (root or base), *svadhishthana* (sacral), *manipura* (solar plexus), *anahata* (heart), *vishuddha* (throat), *ajna* (brow), and *sahasrara* (crown).

Each chakra, other than the crown, is associated with a specific body system and gland. The sacral chakra, for example, controls the digestive system — stomach, liver, gallbladder, and small intestine — together with the adrenal glands, which, among other functions, regulate blood pressure and the body's use of fats. The crown chakra is not restricted to one specific influence but affects the whole person.

In general, the lower three chakras are believed to be concerned with physical energy,

Vishnu chakra
Each chakra is allocated a presiding deity. The svadhishthana, *or sacral, chakra is represented by the god Vishnu, who is often shown holding a conch shell, disk, war club, or lotus.*

the central chakra with the emotions, and the upper three chakras with mental and spiritual energy.

Colors and notes

In addition, each chakra is linked to a particular color of the spectrum, sound frequency, stage of life, and level of consciousness. The sacral chakra, for example, has been assigned the color orange, the note D, the age range 7 months to 18 years, and the consciousness of learning to reach out and grasp, to understand pleasure and pain, and to socialize. In Indian teaching, each chakra is symbolized by a lotus flower with a different number of petals.

In the West the work of color therapists is based on the chakras. A patient's reaction to each color of the spectrum is taken to indicate the strength or weakness of the chakra said to be associated with that color. This in turn, claim supporters, is a pointer to the strength or weakness of the body parts and type of energy related to that chakra — whether physical, mental, spiritual, or emotional.

Oriental chakras
The sites of the living consciousness centers in man.

Coiled serpent

Students of the chakras seek to awaken them. As Naomi Ozaniec describes in *The Elements of the Chakras* (1990), following the teachings of Buddhism or yoga can achieve this. The yoga student may begin by first undertaking *yama* (virtuous conduct), *niyama* (disciplines such as cleanliness and moderation), and commitment to self-discovery and to service to others. Then follows *asana* (meditative postures) and *pranayama* (special breathing techniques). In this way the chakras become well balanced and nadis unrestricted. Energy can then flow freely, followers assert, producing good health and a sense of well-being.

Combined with fasting, chakra-awakening techniques can, it is claimed by experienced practitioners, release a latent inner force known as *kundalini*. Often depicted as a coiled serpent, this is said to shoot up the spine from the root chakra to the crown and to produce an overwhelming feeling of ecstasy, love, and awareness of the Supreme Being. If, however, the preparation for chakra-awakening is in any way faulty — if, for example, breathing is incorrect — the practitioner may find the experience disorientating and may even become temporarily deranged.

Scientific evidence

Western science long tended to dismiss the concept of chakras. But in 1978 Dr. H. Motoyama, a Japanese psychologist, and his American editor R. Brown published *Science and the Evolution of Consciousness: Chakras, Ki and Psi*, which reportedly provided evidence for the existence of the energy centers. In a series of experiments over the years, Dr. Motoyama tested various human subjects by measuring the biolectrical field around each chakra. He discovered that, when certain of these individuals claimed to have awakened their chakras, a copper electrode recorded significant disturbances in the bioelectrical field around them.

But perhaps, in the final analysis, the chakras are a concept that may not be provable scientifically. Naomi Ozaniec writes: "Words alone will not initiate you into the inner meaning of the chakras. You are the only person able to do this by inwardly absorbing [them] through meditation and active participation."

The vishuddha, *or throat, chakra*

ARTIST'S IMPRESSIONS

Although chakras are believed to be centers of pure energy, they have been allocated certain physical characteristics such as color, sound, and age, which enable them to be drawn. In India the chakras are also visualized as lotus flowers with a varying number of petals.

The muladhara, *or root, chakra*

CHAPTER FOUR

HEALTHY INFLUENCES

The New Age movement has rediscovered a number of unusual and ancient therapies. Whatever your ailment, healers using plants and perfumes, colors, or crystals, claim to be able to alleviate it or cure it completely. Most traditional doctors strongly disagree.

All is energy. Albert Einstein, the famed German physicist, helped launch this remarkable concept with his theory of relativity. Recent discoveries in quantum physics have done much to extend and confirm it. Yet there are many different kinds of energy, and almost as many different ideas about what energy might be as there are cultures to express them.

The Chinese, for example, believe in a central life force, and have a special term, *chi*, for the energy that runs through the 12 meridians of the human body. The

Healing oils
Color therapists claim to be able to correct an imbalance in the energy coursing through a person's body. One technique is to massage oil of the correct color into the area of the body connected with the chakra, *or energy center, associated with that color.*

COLOR ANESTHETIC
Dr. Francis J. Kolar of Los Angeles has reportedly used colored lenses to anesthetize his patients during surgery. His colleague, Audrey Kargere, in her book *Color and Personality* (1980), describes how this is done. The patient wears a pair of spectacles with different-colored lenses, and is asked to focus on an electric light bulb about two feet above the head for a count of ten, then close his or her eyes for a further count of ten. The patient repeats this procedure throughout the operation and reportedly becomes insensitive to pain, although still conscious and able to talk.

Higher bodies
In her book *Color Therapy* (1990), Mary Anderson attempts to describe the principle behind this technique: "Correctly prescribed colors promote the attunement to the higher bodies, and people are not aware of their physical bodies when perfectly attuned to the higher bodies. In fact, people who have developed color consciousness are able to withdraw from pain."

Hindus, on the other hand, speak of subtle-energy centers called *chakras* linked by lines of energy called *nadis*.

But is it possible that the energy field of the physical body, in whatever form it might be identified, and other, more subtle energy fields, might be influenced by external forces — for example, the vibrations produced by light, colors, sounds, smells, and perhaps even by the energies of plants?

This is the argument advanced by some New Age therapists who use a range of techniques far beyond the pantheon of orthodox medicine, including: plant essences, aromatherapy, color therapy, and crystal therapy. Nor are these methods new: more than 3,000 years ago the Egyptians were practicing such forms of healing.

New or old, however, these unconventional therapies should not be considered the equal of modern medical procedures and techniques. And they should never replace standard medical diagnosis and treatment.

Bach Flower Remedies
Curiously enough, in modern times, many ancient healing techniques have been rediscovered. Dr. Edward Bach (1886–1936) was a physician specializing in bacteriology at a major London hospital before he began his research into the effects of plant extracts on the human condition. Dr. Bach became convinced of the importance of treating not a particular disease itself but the state of mind that had caused it. And so he created a comprehensive system of 38 Flower Remedies designed to treat a spectrum of human psychological ailments. For mental torture, for example, he recommended the flower of the plant agrimony, for intolerance that of the beech tree, for self-hatred that of the crab apple tree, and so on.

Aromatherapy
Plant extracts are also used in what is known as aromatherapy, supposedly to balance the subtle-energy flows in the body. Modern aromatherapy originated with René-Maurice Gattefosse, a French cosmetic chemist who, in the 1920's, claimed to have rediscovered the healing qualities of plants.

Followers claim that aromatherapy works because the aroma of "essential oils" reaches the brain via the sense of smell and influences the central nervous system. There are smells designed to soothe anxieties (such as bergamot and rose), to relieve depression (sandalwood, verbena), and several that are believed to be aphrodisiacs (jasmine, clary sage).

Color therapy
Someone who is not well might be described as "off color." Color therapists believe that they have the antidote, and claim that they can use colors to restore physical, mental, and emotional health. According to color therapists, each color has its own special qualities, determined by its vibrational frequency. Red, a stimulating color, may be needed to vitalize a tired or lethargic body or spirit,

Bathing in color
In 1989 a House of Sensory Perception, using therapies based on colors, sounds, aromas, textures, and massage, was set up in Denmark to help handicapped children broaden their horizons and extend their sensory experiences.

while calming blue may be used to relieve anxiety and high blood-pressure, reduce inflammation, or soothe pain, adherents of color therapy believe.

Most color therapists base their work on the chakra system of energy centers, according to which each chakra draws a different color-frequency into the body, and distributes it to the organs or nerve centers that will benefit. Color may be administered directly to the central nervous system through the eyes, using lamps with colored filters, or by massage with colored oils that allow the color to be taken into the body through the skin.

THE INFLUENCE OF THE STARS

Astrologers believe that the stars and planets can have a strong influence on a person's character, temperament, and destiny, as well as being a guide to physical strengths and weaknesses, and susceptibility to disease.

THE MOON HAS LONG been associated with mental disturbance — the word lunatic is derived from the Latin *luna*, meaning "moon." But recent research into electrical potential emitted by the body suggests a possible, if still unproven, basis for this connection.

In their book *The Case for Astrology* (1973) John West and Jan Toonder claim that Dr. Leonard Ravitz of Duke University could predict with remarkable accuracy the emotional states of his psychiatric patients at various phases of the moon.

Of greater interest perhaps is the report that hospital patients are more prone to hemorrhage in the first and third phases of the moon. Dr. Edson Andrews, working in Tallahassee, Florida, in the 1960's, claimed that 82 percent of the hemorrhaging in 1,000 cases of tonsillectomy occurred at these times. Other researchers disagree and have been critical of the study.

Cosmic influences

Is it possible that the claims of astrological sages that cosmic influences are important to our health do have some basis in fact? Perhaps, for ancient Egyptian doctors are known to have been especially specific about the times that their remedies were to be administered. And there was a medieval tradition that certain organs of the body existed under the influence of certain planets.

Eva Shaw, a writer on fitness and astrology based in California, believes that the full astrological birth chart should be consulted to provide worthwhile indicators concerning an individual's

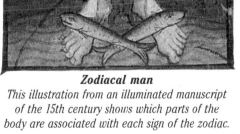

Zodiacal man
This illustration from an illuminated manuscript of the 15th century shows which parts of the body are associated with each sign of the zodiac.

health. In her book *Your Astrological Guide to Fitness* (Mills & Sanderson, 1988) she suggests that certain health tendencies may be associated with specific Sun signs. For convenience, these may be divided into the four elemental groups: fire, earth, air, and water. Fire signs (Aries, Leo, and Sagittarius), she advises, should be wary of heart disease, back complaints, headaches, and fevers. Arians, she believes, are generally too busy to fall ill. Leos, too, have a great deal of vitality but must remember to ease up at times. Sagittarians, because of their love of good food, are reminded that they must watch their weight.

Shaw writes that Earth signs (Taurus, Virgo, and Capricorn) are usually well attuned to their body's needs. Virgoans, however, tend to suffer from bowel and digestive problems, while Taureans have troublesome throats, and Capricorns often fall victim to bone disease and skin complaints.

Physical activity

As for the air signs (Gemini, Libra, and Aquarius), the need here, according to Shaw, is for greater attention to physical activity for a balanced state of health. Geminis might have problems with bronchitis or chest disorders; Librans with kidney or bladder malfunction; and Aquarians with poor circulation or varicose veins.

Water signs (Cancer, Scorpio, and Pisces) tend to be oversensitive and often suffer from stress, Shaw suggests. In Cancerians, this may take the form of gastric disorders. Scorpios need to guard against genitourinary disease, and Pisceans against drink or drug problems, foot trouble, and glandular disorders.

Astrologers also believe that the positions of the stars at the moment of birth are all-important. When they draw up a horoscope, they divide it into 12 "houses," each one corresponding to a different aspect of life. The sixth house governs health. Astrologers even claim to be able to pinpoint potential ailments that might, with medical guidance, be prevented.

CRYSTALS:
LEGACY OF ATLANTIS?

According to crystal therapists, quartz is magical. It can be used to aid meditation, for healing, and as a means of self-defense. It has also been suggested that this is part of a vast store of secret knowledge that has been channeled into a number of civilizations via survivors of the mythical continent of Atlantis. Traditional science takes a dim view of such sparkling promises.

KEEPING QUARTZ UNDER THE PILLOW is said to help you remember your dreams. Use it, too, exponents advise, to help balance inner energies. It can also help your plants to thrive and promote healing in humans and animals.

Such is the litany chanted by supporters of crystal power. And recent years have shown a considerable

> **Valuable knowledge is supposedly just now reemerging as we recover from the cataclysmic changes that followed the destruction of the legendary continent of Atlantis.**

surge of interest in crystals. One explanation for this suggests that valuable knowledge is supposedly just now reemerging as we recover from the cataclysmic changes that followed the destruction, thousands of years ago, of the legendary continent of Atlantis.

There has long been debate concerning the existence of Atlantis and its likely whereabouts. The psychic Edgar Cayce, who claimed he had been an Atlantean in a previous life, also claimed to have visited Atlantis on several occasions during his trances. Cayce reported that he had never

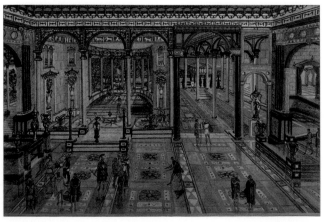

Crystal city?
From Gerald Hargreaves's book, Atalanta, *this artist's reconstruction is an attempt to show what a city on the legendary continent of Atlantis might have looked like.*

Crystal power
According to legend, the continent of Atlantis, engulfed by the sea thousands of years ago, was the cradle of crystal mysteries.

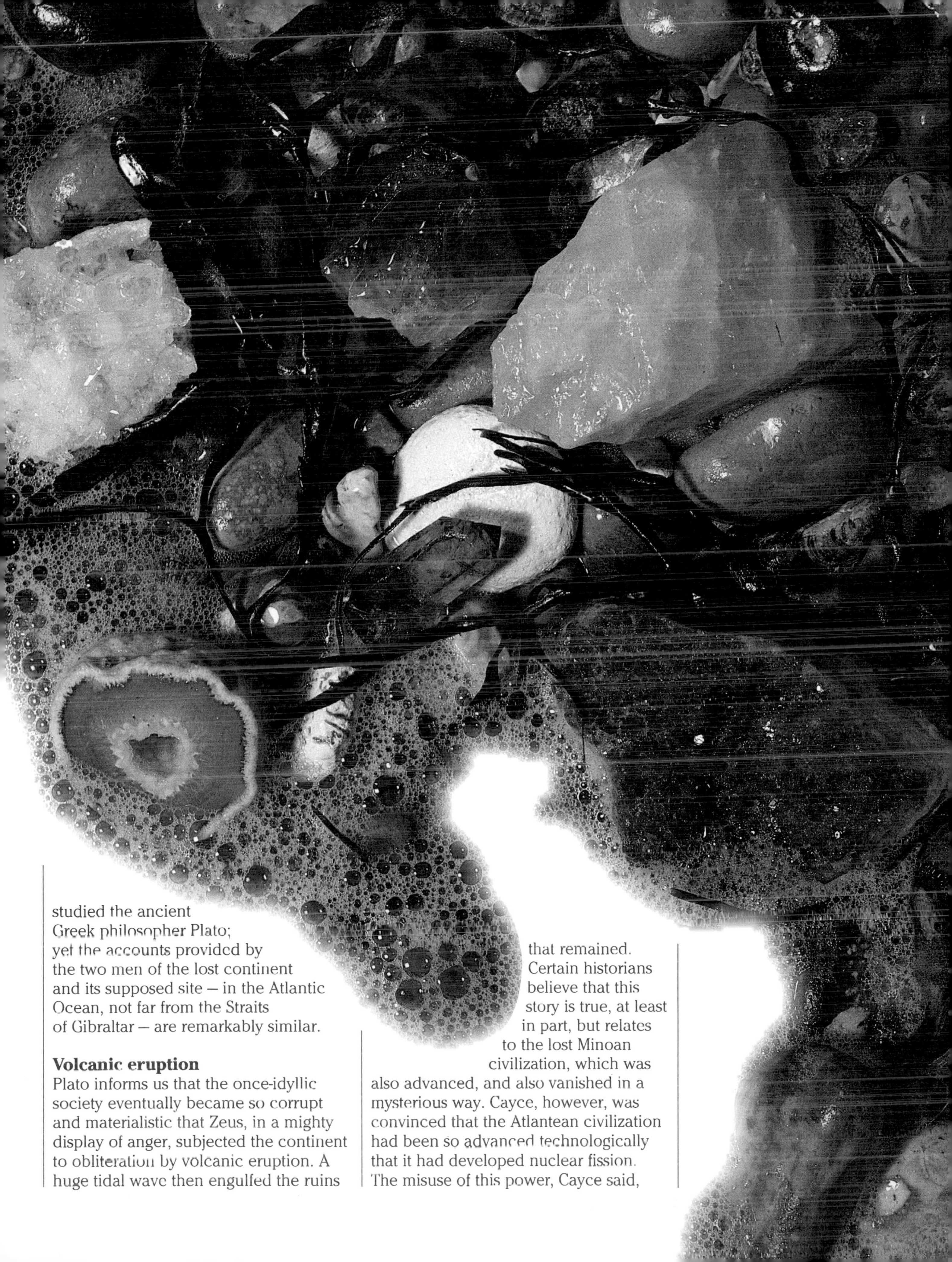

studied the ancient
Greek philosopher Plato;
yet the accounts provided by
the two men of the lost continent
and its supposed site — in the Atlantic
Ocean, not far from the Straits
of Gibraltar — are remarkably similar.

Volcanic eruption

Plato informs us that the once-idyllic
society eventually became so corrupt
and materialistic that Zeus, in a mighty
display of anger, subjected the continent
to obliteration by volcanic eruption. A
huge tidal wave then engulfed the ruins
that remained.
Certain historians
believe that this
story is true, at least
in part, but relates
to the lost Minoan
civilization, which was
also advanced, and also vanished in a
mysterious way. Cayce, however, was
convinced that the Atlantean civilization
had been so advanced technologically
that it had developed nuclear fission.
The misuse of this power, Cayce said,

Scarab amulet
The wearing of special stones as amulets and talismans is a very ancient custom. This winged scarab was worn in ancient Egypt as a lucky charm and as a symbol of resurrection.

MAKING A POWER ROD

Psychic healer and inventor Michael Smith of Colorado suggests making your own power rod, similar to those imagined to have been used by the priests of Atlantis. Take a simple hollow copper tube, about one inch in diameter, and place a copper cap at one end and a quartz crystal at the other. Then bind it spirally with leather. Smith suggests using black leather for psychic protection from outside forces, and green, red, or blue for healing purposes.

The power of thought

According to Smith, if you make it yourself, you can feel the energy emanating from the rod as soon as you pick it up. The rod is charged by the user's own biological field and emotions, and relies upon the power of thought to be effective.

This is not a new idea. In 1796 a Dr. Elisha Perkins patented a similar type of rod made of metal. He called these rods Metallic Tractors and claimed to cure all diseases simply by stroking the patient with them.

Smith has also designed an up-to-date version of the crystal headbands that he believes were worn on Atlantis. These devices are apparently intended to amplify thoughts and ideas, and beam them out in a specific direction.

was what caused the continent suddenly to vanish.

The legend of Atlantis also describes the site as the cradle of crystal mysteries. Flying machines and submarines were crystal powered, so the story goes, as was a system of domestic electricity. The priestly class used crystals for various purposes: to heal, to transmit messages, and to alter the psychological makeup of criminals. It was said that the Atlantean women held real power, since they possessed the greatest mastery of the mysterious qualities of quartz.

Ornamental amulets

But such ancient wisdom, it seems, did not disappear entirely when Atlantis fell, for certain experts in the science of crystals managed to reach Egypt. (The pyramids are thought by some to be replicas of the great temple of Atlantis.) And, apparently, crystals were used not just as ornamental amulets, but for the purpose of creating harmony between mind, body, and spirit. Quartz, the ancient Egyptians believed, had the power to help them see the way to eternal life.

Among the aboriginal peoples of Australia and New Guinea, too, quartz

has long been used for divination, and in rainmaking ceremonies. In other parts of the world, substantial quantities of quartz are found below major megalithic sites — Stonehenge, for example. This appears to be more than coincidence, and the special qualities of quartz, adherents say, may have held particular attraction for primitive peoples.

American Indian tradition refers to the teachings of Atlantis being passed on to their ancestors in ancient times. The Yuman speakers of southern and Baja California consider the quartz crystal a "live rock." Quartz has been found there at sites dating back 8,000 years.

Generators of power

Psychic healer and inventor Michael Smith of Colorado studied for some time with an American Indian medicine man who used crystals in his work. Smith is convinced that the lost continent of Atlantis reached a far higher stage of civilization than our own, and he has been working to re-create its crystal artifacts. Smith has suggested that the staff of Moses — used to part the Red Sea — may have been a crystal-based "power rod." This highly speculative theory might explain why, throughout history, priests and magicians are often depicted carrying wands; they may have been more than just symbols of power.

According to Smith, those in power on Atlantis would have wielded a power rod. He claims, somewhat grandly, that such a thing can be made today, and can

be used to influence the weather, encourage plant growth, improve health, change traffic lights, affect computer systems, and promote business profits and even world peace. Smith makes a number of hard to

Rocks of religion
Each of the 12 tribes of Israel is represented by one of the gemstones in this ceremonial breastplate of the Jewish high priest.

substantiate claims, for example: traffic lights reportedly have been "frozen" at the same signal for up to eight minutes by use of a power rod; and he says he used his to cure a woman with ovarian cysts in just 25 minutes.

Strange skull

Another confirmed believer in the Atlantis legend was the archeologist F. A. Mitchell-Hedges. And the most intriguing

> Many believe the skull to have mystical properties. Some people have noticed an aura around it, and others say they have heard chimes and even the sound of human voices emanating from it.

crystal object in existence is probably the Mitchell-Hedges Skull, a large piece of solid crystal found by his daughter Anna in 1927 during their excavations at Mayan sites in British Honduras in South America. The size of a human skull, the Mitchell-Hedges skull is thought to have taken 300 years to produce, so hard is the quartz from which it was carved. Yet there seem to be no tool marks on it at all.

A distinct aura

Many believe the skull to have mystical properties. At times the frontal lobe appears to turn opaque. Some people say they have noticed an aura around it, and others say they have heard chimes and even the sound of human voices emanating from it. Some authorities have suggested that it is more than 50,000 years old, and that it was transported to the Americas by the Atlanteans, if indeed they existed. In any case, several other crystal skulls have also been found in this region.

A CRYSTAL CRITIC

Barbara G. Walker takes a skeptical view of the modern cult of crystal healing in *The Book of Sacred Stones* (1989). She is suspicious of the fact that many so-called healers have only the most rudimentary knowledge of the properties of the minerals and stones they use. For example, some appear not to know that gemstones are insoluble in water, for they claim that by immersing a gem in water for a short period, gemstone elixirs can be produced that may prove efficacious in treating disease. Walker also emphasizes the fact that of all the books on crystal healing, no two recommend the same stones and techniques for treating a particular illness.

The placebo effect

Walker suggests that if people do feel better after a crystal cure, it may be due to their having the undivided attention of a "healer" for longer than they might see their doctor. She also quotes the 10th-century Syrian physician Qusta ibn-Luqa on the placebo effect, which was apparently well known even in his day: "The state of mind affects the state of the body. Sometimes belief in the curative value of a prophylactic is enough."

Extravagant claims

Walker's scathing attack continues: "It is claimed...that all stones emit sounds that have a great potential for healing. When did anyone ever hear a sound emitted by a stone, or when did any sound cure a disease? It is claimed that crystals cure bursitis by 'brealing [sic] down the calcification deposits that occur in various joints,' although bursitis has nothing to do with calcification. It is claimed that double terminated quartz crystals placed under each eye can reverse the aging process. It is claimed that crystals affect a second, 'causal' heart that is located on the right side of the chest. This world-shaking discovery that each of us has two hearts has been somehow overlooked in centuries of anatomy studies."

Mexican crystal skull
A skull of rock crystal, nearly 8 1/2 inches long, probably dating from the Aztec period, c. A.D. 1300–1500.

THE HEALING STONES

Although the use of crystals has become a widely practiced New Age healing technique, doctors believe crystals do no good. Crystal therapists like Caroline Boddie disagree. Here she describes how she uses crystals in what remains a controversial therapy.

"CRYSTALS ARE A TOOL created by the Great Creative Force that made all things and beings on this planet. Crystals are subtle in their energy and powerful in their results. The electromagnetic energy of crystals is in perfect harmony with the bio-electromagnetic field of all living things. It is this field and the pure 'Light Essence' of crystals that I work with to bring change in the spiritual, mental, emotional, and physical aspects of an individual. The energy of the crystals permeates these four aspects producing sometimes small, sometimes large changes.

"One of the many ways of using crystals is to have a person wear one (after having cleansed and cleared it) around his or her neck between the throat and heart chakras.

Auric field
"Wearing a crystal also extends your auric field so that it extends approximately 18–25 feet beyond the physical body. A clear crystal will help to balance, harmonize, and bring peace to all those who walk into this field.

"I must, however, warn you of the power of crystals. A conscious effort should be made to bring your thinking to a balanced place, as you influence more people than ever before when you wear a crystal. Each morning balance your energies and see the 'White Light' or 'God Light' entering your body at the crown and traveling down through the chakras to your feet.

An aura scan
"This is a technique for balancing the body's electrical energies. Place a crystal in your right hand with the point facing away from you and toward the body to be scanned. Begin scanning

Amethyst

Agate

Smoky quartz

THE TOP 10 CRYSTALS

Crystal therapist Caroline Boddie describes her 10 favorite crystals and explains how she uses them in her work.

Clear quartz
"Clear to milky in color. Clear quartz amplifies mind power and also balances the physical, emotional, mental, and spiritual bodies equally, thereby creating wholeness in all aspects of self. Students should hold a clear quartz point in their left hand while studying in order to improve retention and clarity. Use clear quartz to be more open and clear thinking. Wear it and meditate with it."

Amethyst
"Lilac to deep purple in color. Amethyst takes the spiritual essence that is you and transforms it, raising it to a higher spiritual energy. It is a store of transmutation, wisdom, love, and protection. It opens the crown chakra, allowing in divine knowledge."

Green quartz
"Pale green to very deep green in color (sometimes mistaken for jade). Also known as Aventurine. Green quartz is the great healing stone of the quartz family. It can be worn as a pendant or placed directly on the afflicted area, for example, an arthritic joint."

Agate
"This crystal comes in many colors. Agate was used in ancient times to heal the physical body and to protect the etheric body from psychic attack. Today it is still used all over the Middle East and Orient for the same reason. Wear an agate pendant to protect yourself from any negative thoughts."

Smoky quartz
"Very light to almost black in color. Suppliers may irradiate amethyst and clear quartz to make it smoky. Only natural smoky quartz will give the right effect. It is the great grounding stone of the quartz family and is for dreamers who find it difficult to function in everyday life. It also absorbs negativity."

Rutilated quartz

"Clear quartz with gold wire inside of it. Rutilated quartz amplifies mind power. It balances the throat, brow, and crown chakras. It is a powerful quartz to meditate with as it opens you up to divine guidance. You can also wear it as a pendant."

Rutilated quartz

Tourmilated quartz

"Clear quartz that has black tourmaline inside of it. Tourmilated quartz amplifies mind power. It balances the solar plexus, sacral, and root chakras. It works at the root chakra to balance impotence, frigidity, nymphomania, and satyriasis. It is also good for prostate problems. Wear it or meditate with it."

Rose quartz

"Very pale to deepest pink in color. Madagascar quartz is the finest gem-quality rose quartz. Rose quartz balances the emotional field. It opens up the heart chakra and brings in love. It should, therefore, always be worn near the heart chakra. A large chunk of rose quartz should be placed in every child's room for its calming effect. Just holding a medium-sized chunk in the left hand helps to cope with stress. Rose quartz can also be used to help in meditation."

Rose quartz

Carnelian

"Light to dark orange in color. Carnelian balances the solar plexus, sacral, and root chakras. It is particularly good for blood filtration areas such as liver and spleen. It also works very well in quieting the symptoms of PMS (pre menstrual syndrome). It should be taped to the lower abdomen as soon as symptoms appear."

Citrine

"Pale yellow to deep golden in color. Citrine in its raw state balances the solar plexus, sacral, and root chakras. Also good for the prostate. It is the only quartz that changes its properties when tumbled or polished. Citrine then balances the throat, brow, and crown chakras. It also opens the crown chakra and is therefore good to meditate with."

Citrine

at the head, working downward toward the feet, keeping the crystal about two inches away from the body. When you come to an area that seems cold or hot, or when you feel a vibration in your hand, turn the crystal counterclockwise and touch the tip of the crystal to the center of that area. Continue down the body front and back until you have balanced all areas that appear to be out of sync. This leaves the body relaxed and at peace.

"I have seen many people suffering from nervous conditions. For these people I recommend a full body treatment. This entails an aura scan, neurological balancing, circulatory balancing, and colored quartz stone balancing. Such a treatment lasts about 40 minutes and is too intricate to describe fully here.

Practical healing

"Using this treatment, I dissolved a bone spur in my foot. After seven treatments on a manic depressive, he was on one-half medication (with his doctor's consent) and getting better. Today he no longer needs medication or counseling. I could fill this book with similar examples.

"I like to meditate with crystals. Sit holding a quartz crystal in your left hand with the point facing in toward you and you will achieve the correct alpha brain wave state.

"Over the years, thousands of people have learned how to use crystals from me. All have had positive results. Use them with respect and knowledge. To do otherwise is dangerous. Crystals bring light and wisdom to all who use them."

Beyond the pale

Although crystal healers are genuinely convinced of the success of their methods, medical doctors and even others in the alternative health movement are not. They can find no evidence that crystals can cure disease or improve health and fitness in any way. Doctors have even suggested that relying on crystal healing might be harmful, for it could prevent those in need of modern medical assistance from receiving the treatment they need.

In Search of Serenity

It is now generally accepted, even in conventional medical circles, that stress can be a contributory factor in the onset of some diseases. The New Age movement offers a range of techniques to help ease the strains of modern living.

THE PREOCCUPATION OF NEW AGERS with the goal of positive health has led to their popularizing a number of techniques to promote serenity in the individual. The aim is to locate what they describe as that still point within — where the self is grounded and centered in the midst of outer bustle and chaos.

In New Age terms, the fact that many people do not feel totally healthy or do not feel that they are doing a good job with their lives (and don't expect the future to be better) indicates that they haven't yet discovered that the answers lie within — or that they don't know how to begin the inward journey toward self.

Relaxation

The first thing to do, adherents say, is to relax. As people progress through life, they tend to lose the knack. In recent years researchers have become very interested in relaxation. One of the most influential is Dr. Herbert Benson of Harvard Medical School, who has studied the body's fight-or-flight response. Unfortunately, this mechanism tends to be triggered by the stresses of modern life. The effects of this all too common response (raised blood pressure and increased heart rate, pupil dilation, massive blood flow to muscles) create considerable strain on the body.

Dr. Benson discovered that the body has its own antidote — the relaxation response, which slows the heart rate, decreases adrenalin and cholesterol, and produces other beneficial effects. With practice it is possible to make this the normal response to stress.

Relaxation, however, requires the stilling of the mind and the loosening of the body. And it is often practiced in conjunction with other techniques, such as meditation, visualization, and affirmation.

Affirmation

One popular technique for enhancing relaxation is the creative focusing of thought through repeated statements of affirmation. Affirmations help to develop new thoughts, attitudes, and beliefs, making it easier to change a lifestyle — make a career move, a change in self-image, or a health improvement through a change in diet or exercise regime.

Therapists usually teach that an affirmation should be phrased in the present tense, and that it should be a positive statement. For example, "I will not eat fattening foods" is not helpful. Far better is: "Everything I eat turns to health and beauty," or: "My body processes everything I eat to my correct weight of 133 pounds." These positive statements set a tone of optimism and increase self-esteem.

Low self-esteem

Louise L. Hay, holder of an honorary doctorate in medicine, has, through her book *Heal Your Body* (1989), popularized the technique of affirmation. When she was diagnosed as having vaginal cancer, she came to the conclusion that this was the result of a childhood full of mental, physical, and sexual abuse, a childhood that had left her full of anger,

She put off surgery and began to affirm her right to self-love, to the love and support of the universe, and to perfect health. Six months later the doctors reportedly could find no trace of cancer.

resentment, and low self-esteem. She believed that unless she could clear from her mind and body the pattern that was causing the cancer, surgery would never be able to help.

She put off surgery and began to affirm her right to self-love, to the love and support of the universe, and to perfect health. Six months later the doctors reportedly could find no trace of cancer. (It is important to remember, however, that despite such success stories, New Age techniques should be considered as complementary, and should never replace conventional medical diagnosis and treatment.)

Hay's research pinpoints the diseases she believes are caused by particular feelings — fear, anger, frustration, rejection, and guilt. She teaches that the thoughts that produce these negative emotions can be changed by

BRAIN WAVES

The varying electrical rhythms of the brain, as measured by an EEG (electroencephalograph) machine, can be divided into four categories, each of which is associated with a particular state of awareness. Beta waves have a frequency of over 13Hz (cycles per second) and signify that the brain is in a state of normal waking awareness. Alpha waves (8–13Hz) seem to be present during all the higher levels of awareness, and when the mind is very calm and the body is relaxed. Theta waves (4–7Hz) occur during meditation and at times of creative inspiration. Delta waves (0.5–3.5Hz) signify the rhythm of sleep, but also occur in waking people in response to new ideas, and in healers and psychics.

The Mind Mirror

There is a type of EEG machine called the Mind Mirror that gives a frequency analysis of the rhythms of both sides of a subject's brain. This was used in early research on the different properties of the left- and right-hand sides of the brain. It is still used as an aid to relaxation, and to monitor the patterns associated with different levels of meditation.

Business brains

Anna Wise, of San Francisco, uses the Mind Mirror for personnel recruitment. She claims to have isolated the combination of brain waves most suited to a range of executive positions: managing director, finance director, marketing director, for example. Prospective employers may subject job candidates to a Mind Mirror test to assess their suitability for a particular job.

Nepalese mandala
Meditational aids are not a new idea. The effect of some of the modern New Age brain-stimulation equipment has been compared to that of Buddhist or Hindu mandalas. These symbolic representations of the universe have been used for centuries to focus the brain during meditation.

affirmations. Her affirmations stress the importance of loving the self, the value of individuals who learn to take control of their lives, and the significance of the notion that the universe provides everyone with everything they need.

A visual approach

Those who work with visualization, however, point out that words are only symbolic. Most people concentrate on images that are positive, visualizing, for example, not the weight to be lost but the slender person who has lost it.

Visualization involves creating mental sense impressions (which may involve sound, taste, smell, and touch as well as vision) in order to make changes in your health and performance. Sometimes visualization may be done symbolically; for instance, a tension headache may be relieved by picturing a band around the head loosening and falling away.

O. Carl Simonton, M.D., runs the Simonton Cancer Care Center in Pacific Palisades, California. He has spent much of his career treating cancer patients,

and has concluded that complementary therapies have a place alongside conventional medical treatment. In his book, *Getting Well Again* (1986), he expounds his theories about conquering cancer through positive thinking.

Simonton's best-known theory is that it is beneficial to tell patients to imagine their white blood cells killing cancer

> ## A tension headache may be relieved by picturing a band around the head loosening and falling away.

cells. He now suggests that patients should also visualize the cancer cells being "whisked away." Most therapists who use this type of suggestion say that the patient should visualize the area of the body in a healthy state, after healing.

But Simonton's theories have been the subject of medical debate. Dr. Barrie Cassileth, director of psychosocial programs at the University of Pennsylvania Cancer Center in Philadelphia, stated categorically in a 1985 issue of the *New England Journal of Medicine* that a patient's attitude had no effect on survival rates or recurrence of cancer in a study conducted on a sample of 359 patients.

Effective visualization

According to its supporters, you need to be relaxed to achieve effective visualization; and the effect of the relaxation in itself will be beneficial. Relaxation also produces alpha waves, slower brainwaves than those used in active thought, which leave the mind open to positive suggestions.

Meditation is another step on the inward journey to self. It has been described as "dynamic relaxation." Yogis have a

▶ PAGE 96

SHORTCUTS TO NIRVANA?

A number of machines have been devised in recent years in an attempt to speed the psychic traveler on his or her inward journey to calmness, peace, and serenity.

IT IS NOW KNOWN that the electrochemical patterns of the brain may be affected in varying degrees by external stimuli (lights, sounds, movements, etc.). It appears possible, therefore, at least in theory, to guide the mind into any chosen state and, with the right kind of stimulation, shift the brain into a higher gear. Much equipment has been devised in the effort to harness this potential. Most such devices consist of a stimuli-producing unit with a control panel and electrodes that connect the user to the system.

It should be remembered, however, that all such devices are experimental and may be costly. In addition there is little if any scientific proof that they are effective.

The Synchro-Energizer, for example, which was invented by psychiatrist and medical researcher Denis Gorges, comes with headphones and goggles, and stimulates the subject by means of electronic sounds, New Age music, and flickering white lights. The experimental device's control panel permits the user to manipulate a number of variables in order to influence brain-wave frequency and heart rate, and to focus on one or both hemispheres of the brain. Users of the machine report increased mental clarity, creative thinking, and vivid mental imagery, with a lessening of tension and anxiety. A group-therapy version for up to 32 people is also available.

The Star Chamber

Like the Synchro-Energizer, the Star Chamber is another highly speculative machine. It emits sounds of different frequencies and uses flashing lights to supposedly induce a state of well-being. In this case, however, the lights are emitted from the ceiling of the chamber and projected all over the body.

The Hemi-Sync machine was devised by Robert Monroe, a businessman reportedly prone to OBE's — out-of-body-experiences. He experimented with the effects of sound vibrations on the brain, and found that with his FFR (Frequency Following Response) machine

Mental workout
In the Altered States Mind Gym in California, it is possible to try out a range of equipment designed to enhance creativity, powers of memory, and decisiveness. The machines shown here are (left to right): a Synchro-Energizer, a Mind Mirror, a Star Chamber, and a massage chair.

he could, he says, reproduce for others the vibratory state that might trigger an OBE, if such states exist. Another unproven device, the Graham Potentializer, continuously revolves the subject (lying on a bed) through what is reported to be a specially generated electromagnetic field. It has been designed, its creators report, with the goal of producing increased mental energy and clarity. Users claim that it produces a meditative experience.

A sense of euphoria

California neurobiologist Dr. Daniel Kirsch, the inventor of the Alpha Stim machine, says the electric currents it sends to the brain create a state he describes as "electronarcosis." Dr. Kirsch believes that this is a state that produces relaxation and heightened awareness, and that it brings with it a sense of euphoria.

Interesting as these inventions may be, it is important to remember that they are highly experimental, may do nothing, and in themselves cannot enhance mental powers. If they work at all they may do so by harnessing techniques of sensory deprivation to help the mind make use of powers that it already has.

high level of control over all their mental and physical functions. How they achieve this control has fueled much research in the United States and Britain. At the height of his popularity in the mid-1970's, Maharishi Mahesh Yogi, who brought his method of transcendental meditation (TM) to the West from India, invited researchers from several reputable institutions, including Harvard and UCLA, to examine the effects of meditation, and showed that he could alter body processes — heartbeat, rate of oxygen consumption, etc. — at will.

Successful meditation involves first achieving deep physical relaxation and then attaining a mental state in which the mind eases its hold on thinking and feeling. It experiences instead a state of pure awareness that is, the maharishi says, the essential nature of the mind. It is described by psychologist Lawrence Le Shan as "like coming home."

Meditating monk
Buddhist monk in front of a temple in Yangon, in the Union of Myanmar (formerly Rangoon, Burma).

Religious thought
A Japanese Zen Buddhist monk deep in meditation.

Zen meditation

Meditation practice usually takes the form of focusing on one thing to the exclusion of all others. In the case of TM this is a mantra (a chanted sound) devised for each individual by the instructor. People can meditate on a number of different things, for instance an object such as a candle flame or a flower, or a rythmic sound such as one's heartbeat or breathing. Zazen (Zen) meditation does not focus on any one thing; instead it allows any thought that might arise to pass through the mind without attention.

One means of helping or assisting the making of such an inward journey is available in the form of what is known as a flotation tank. This is a small shallow pool, which has been light- and sound-proofed. It is filled with warm water into which huge quantities of Epsom salts have been added. The salts allow the floater's body to lie almost completely on the surface. Thus the floater experiences almost total sensory deprivation.

As a result, stress factors — heart rate, blood pressure, the release of stress-related hormones — are all reduced and the body's relaxation response begins to operate; endorphins, substances that reduce pain and can induce mild euphoria, are reportedly producd and released; powers of creative visualization also greatly increase, it is said, as do powers of memory, and problem-solving ability.

> "Since the mind ordinarily remains attuned to the senses...and their monitoring of the external...it misses or fails to appreciate its own essential nature, just as the eyes are unable to see themselves."
>
> **Maharishi Mahesh Yogi**

Controlled studies

These effects have been monitored in rigorously controlled studies at the universities of Texas, Colorado, British Columbia, and at Stanford and Ohio universities. It has been found that such beneficial effects may last for weeks.

AUTOSUGGESTION

"Learn to cure yourselves; you can do so; I have never cured anyone. The power is within you yourselves; call upon your spirit, make it act for your spiritual and mental good, and it will come, it will cure you, you will be strong and happy."
Emile Coué

THE SELF-HEALING CONCEPT called autosuggestion was developed by a 19th-century French pharmacist, Emile Coué. Couéism, as it was first called, gained widespread popularity throughout the world at the beginning of the 20th century.

Pharmacist turned healer

Coué believed that the human mind possessed deep reserves of untapped energy and that this power could be released to heal the mind and body by using simple forms of verbal repetition. Coué claimed that profound changes, both psychological and physical, could be achieved by this self-administered technique

Coué had first become interested in the healing power of the mind when he worked as an apothecary in Provence in the south of France in the 1880's. When one of his patients was cured of a long-standing complaint by a newly patented medicine, he analyzed its composition and found it contained nothing more than colored water. If colored water cured the patient's ailment, Coué reasoned, then some other healing agent must be at work.

Power of the mind

In France at the end of the 19th century, there was a medical vogue for something known as heterosuggestion, or what we would recognize today as hypnosis, in treating all forms of illness. The leading exponent of this was a French physician, Dr. A. A. Liébeault, who was treating patients successfully with hypnosis in the town of Nancy. After observing Liébeault's clinical work, Coué concluded that the process he himself had developed, called autosuggestion, could be even more successful in healing patients.

Coué believed that a patient's subconscious mind was constantly at war with his or her will, and in this struggle the subconscious would always win. A patient might have the willpower to become well but would not if his or her subconscious feared it was not possible. Succumbing to the sickness then became a self-fulfilling prophecy.

Coué believed that it was possible to "educate" the subconscious mind. This was achieved by concentrating, clearing the mind

of all distracting mental "chatter" and everyday concerns. To do this, he borrowed the ancient Hindu technique of repeating sacred phrases known as mantras. Coué's health-giving incantation was "Every day in every way, I am getting better and better." Nowadays a number of doctors acknowledge the therapeutic value of autosuggestion. In its modern guise it is known as affirmation, and forms part of several holistic therapies for cancer patients.

Willpower
Emile Coué examines a patient.

Good Vibrations

Vibrations, emanations, and energy fields are just some of the terms used by New Age "healers" to describe the forces they claim to work with — forces, they say, that lie beyond the realm of science.

CAROLINE MYSS OF NEW HAMPSHIRE claims to be able to diagnose illness without seeing the patient. Doctors hundreds of miles away have called her to assist them in evaluating sick people. Working from only the name and age of the patient, Myss gives a complete report on any significant disease that she senses is present. Some doctors claim that she is at least as accurate as traditional means of diagnosis, while others do not believe that her work is useful.

Not surprisingly, it is difficult for those accustomed to traditional methods of observation and diagnosis to accept such alternative approaches. Some practitioners of alternative methods claim to have special powers of awareness that enable them to see inside the human body or to view subjects miles from them. They claim that they can detect "vibrations" not yet recognized by orthodox science. Critics of these practices claim that they are without scientific basis.

Radiesthesia and radionics

Two of the more common methods of alternative diagnosis are called radiesthesia and radionics. Both are based on the theory that all forms of matter emit certain invisible "vibrations," or "emanations."

Radiesthetic theory states that each organ of the body produces a different vibration. This makes it possible to tune into the emanations of, for example, the heart, lungs, or small intestine. Furthermore, practitioners claim, these emanations change in predictable ways as the organ's health deteriorates.

Followers of this theory claim that they can assess a person's state of health by using a pendulum and a drop of dried blood. The pendulum is held over a photograph of a patient or a drawing of the human body (one that outlines the major organ systems), that is situated next to the dried blood. When the pendulum is held over a particular diseased organ, its swinging may change from the pattern it might normally follow when positioned over a healthy portion of the body.

A higher intelligence

Radiesthetic theory assumes that all persons have in them a kind of "higher intelligence," which knows about the health status of the body and what it needs to repair itself. According to this highly theoretical approach, it is therefore possible to ask specific questions of this intelligence, such as: "Are the lungs healthy? Is there emphysema present?"

The use of a radionics machine is more complex, yet its operations are based, supporters claim, on the general principles and theory of radiesthesia. The first radionic instrument was developed in the early 20th century by Albert Abrams, M.D., M.A., of San Francisco. Since then it has been refined and modified by many other believers including a Californian chiropractor, Ruth Drown, and an English civil engineer, George de la Warr.

Inside the supposed diagnostic instrument — or the black box as some call it — is a complex series of coils and

---

The diagnostician tunes in by focusing on a photograph, a drop of dried blood, or a hair sample from the patient.

---

wires, all connected to a magnet that is sometimes powered by batteries. On the outside of the radionic instrument are several dials. One or more dials are used to tune in to specific organs such as the eyes or gallbladder, and the dials may be used to record the force of the emanations, or the degree of health, adherents believe, that is present in that particular organ system.

Health emanations

The diagnostician tunes in by focusing on a photograph, a drop of dried blood, or a hair sample from the patient. Although radionic devices differ, the operator usually rubs his or her finger on a rub plate, which may be a piece of rubber, smooth metal, or glass. As the operator moves the selector dial to determine the degree of health, at the same time posing the question mentally, there is supposed to be a change in the degree of friction between the finger and the plate. When the correct setting on the dial is reached, the finger seems to stick, adherents claim, indicating the specific health reading for that organ.

In *Report on Radionics* (1988), the English radionics practitioner Edward Russell gives the results of tests with the

♦ PAGE 102

AURA OF HEALTH

Scientists acknowledge that every human being emits energy that is made up of radiations from the chemicals and cells in our body. Aura therapists believe that this energy has a visible form, and that its colors reveal a person's physical and mental well-being.

FROM ANCIENT TIMES psychically gifted people have claimed to be able to see auras of colored light glowing around a person's body. Depictions of auras are found in Australian aboriginal cave paintings and carved on American Indian totem poles. From medieval times, European religious paintings depicted people of high spiritual standing with their heads encircled with a halo of shining white or yellow light. Today, some alternative healers, known as aura therapists, believe it is possible to interpret auras to diagnose physical sickness and a person's state of mind. Orthodox medicine, however, does not accept such convictions.

A scientific explanation

In 1909 an English doctor, Walter J. Kilner of St. Thomas's Hospital, London, discovered that by looking through glass screens that had been coated with dicyanin dye, he could see an aura that appeared like a shimmering haze extending several inches around the subject's body. Another scientist, biologist Oscar Bagnell at Cambridge University, reportedly developed this work, showing that the brighter an aura, the healthier an individual might be. Conventional medical opinion, however, remained unconvinced about what, if anything, such auras might reveal.

Prenatal aura

In his book *The Outline of Spiritual Healing* (1970) Gordon Turner, a British "spiritual healer," described what he said were his experiences in seeing auras. He claimed that he could see the aura of a baby in its mother's womb six months before birth. He also claimed that children possessed very definite auras. These appeared to be made up of only one or two colors, he maintained, and the auric field appeared to be closer to the body than in an adult.

Turner also recorded what he reportedly had seen happen to an auric field when a person died in his presence. As the person was dying, Turner asserts, the auric field lost its color and became a dull gray. When all the vital signs had ceased, however, Turner claimed that the aura gradually changed in color, turning from gray to a dull blue before becoming a brilliant azure blue. Suddenly, he says, the room filled with all the

colors of the rainbow. This spectacular collection of colors then apparently exploded in front of his eyes and disappeared in a bright flash of light.

Healing colors

Aura therapists also believe that every time we meet someone we respond to that person's aura at an unconscious level. Such therapists also claim they are able to diagnose an individual's physical and mental health by examining the aura. Aura therapists make their diagnoses based on the seven colors in the aura

> **Aura therapists believe that every time we meet someone we respond to that person's aura at an unconscious level.**

spectrum. These colors are said to be created by the radiation emissions from the cells and chemicals in the body. The aura spectrum is divided into primary and secondary colors. The primary colors are red, yellow, and blue. The four secondary colors are orange, green, indigo, and violet.

◆ Red, according to aura therapists, is associated with life and physical vigor. An excess of red is interpreted as indicating a selfish or materialistic person. In terms of health, red is associated with excretory functions and the sex glands.
◆ Yellow is the color of optimism and intellect. Pale yellow is interpreted as indicating indecisiveness. Yellow is associated with the digestive system, reproduction, and childbirth.
◆ Blue is associated with idealism and integrity. It is the color associated with the thyroid, the ear, nose, and throat, breathing, and speech.
◆ Orange indicates energy and good health. This color is associated with the adrenal glands, sexual functioning, and the spleen. Too much orange can indicate selfishness.
◆ Green is the color that represents nature and to aura therapists, healing. It indicates a lively personality and is associated with the heart and the circulatory system.
◆ Indigo is the color of intuition and indicates psychic abilities. When indigo predominates in an aura, it signifies calmness. Indigo is associated with the pituitary gland and the lymphatic system.
◆ Violet is the color associated with spiritual enlightenment, wisdom, and love.
◆ Black or gray are colors associated with ignorance. They also indicate that the aura has been damaged in some way through stress or illness.
◆ White is the color that indicates that health and spirit are perfectly balanced.

AN AURA AT BEDTIME

The following technique, devised by an English clairvoyant, S. G. J. Ousley, in the 1940's, is supposed to enable anyone to see an auric field. When going to bed at night, take an ordinary iron magnet with you. Turn the light out and get into bed and relax completely for a minute or two. Empty your head of any distracting thoughts. It is important that you make your mind as passive as possible. Now place the magnet under the bedclothes, and gaze steadily at it. In order to do this it may be necessary to locate its position with your hands. After a few moments of gazing steadily at the magnet, you should be able to see the auric haze around the two poles of the magnet. Auric consultants believe that the more defined the aura that you may see — if, indeed, you see anything at all — the greater your clairvoyant abilities.

Colorful thoughts

If you still fail to see an aura, the following visualization exercise may help. All this technique requires is concentration and an envelope. Sit down in a quiet room, and visualize a globe of light that is constantly changing color. The colors move from red to orange, yellow, green, blue, indigo, and violet.

Concentrate on each of the colors in your head. After a few minutes look at the envelope in your hand and visualize an imaginary color within it. Ousley recommended this exercise to his subjects, and claimed that he found that it trained them to be able to see a person's auric haze with little difficulty.

Pendulum power
Radiesthetic practitioners use different techniques for diagnosis, although the general principle remains the same. The variety of methods is reflected in the variety of radiesthetic pendulums shown here.

In full swing
Radiesthetic practitioner David Tansley demonstrates his own technique with a pendulum over a treatment chart.

general public. Some 40 percent seemed unable to use the device.

Although many seemed to get some results, only 30 percent produced any meaningful results, Russell claimed.

Another series of experiments used radionic devices with internal wires and circuits disconnected and the power source removed. Yet many operators reportedly achieved the same readings on these false machines as they did on the original models. This may support the point — if radionics is effective — that the operator is the machine, and the elaborate sets of dials are simply a way of focusing his or her psychic abilities.

How accurate is radionics claimed to be? One expert who has worked in the field for 30 years states that reliable operators can achieve 75 to 80 percent accuracy on a consistent basis. But a British Medical Association report, *Alternative Therapy* (1986), was skeptical about the technique. "'Energy patterns' are also fundamental to the belief of those who practise radionics....In our view, reliance on descriptions of energy flows to account for the effect of alternative therapies, in the absence of precise definitions or an explicit (let alone systematic) theoretical framework, is no more than dogmatic metaphysics ....We understand the appeal of such concepts to those who wish to reject what they see as the materialism of scientific medicine, but we do not believe that these methods are of any therapeutic value in themselves."

Therapeutic touch

Another alternative method of diagnosis is therapeutic touch. The practice of this goes back many centuries, but it has recently been popularized by Dolores Krieger, professor emeritus of nursing at New York University.

This diagnostic process — or "assessment" as Krieger prefers to call it — consists of the practitioner passing his or her hands over the surface of the patient's body. The hands need not actually touch the skin; they usually pass one to three or more inches above the surface. Practitioners of therapeutic touch report that they feel "rough spots," or "heat," or "cold," or "thickness" in the areas where there is disease in the body. People experienced in the use of the method claim it is all they need to know to begin alleviating the problem.

Subtle energy

Practitioners of this method claim that the physical form is surrounded and penetrated by a subtle body of energy. This energy, they say, cannot be measured by modern science, but "sensitive" individuals can feel it as they pass their hands through it. They claim that this energy field is what organizes and vitalizes the physical body. Thus, changes in this subtle energy (congestions, deficiencies, breaks, blockage of flow) produce illness in the physical body.

In her book, *The Therapeutic Touch* (1986), Dolores Krieger suggests that it is not just a diagnostic technique, but may also relieve the symptoms of some ailments. Krieger reports success in stopping colic in infants and acute asthmatic attacks in adults. One test of experienced and skilled practitioners of this technique reportedly obtained about 80 percent accuracy in their evaluations.

Intuitive diagnosis

Perhaps the most common type of alternative diagnosis makes use of intuition, or "psychic" senses. Intuitives may be given only the name and age of a patient, perhaps a photo or a signature, to help them "find" the subject.

The typical intuitive thinks or reflects on the subject and then supposedly begins to receive information. This may consist of the image of the person or of a diseased area of the body. Other intuitives just receive mental impressions, such as: "There is a tumor in the upper middle colon." Still others might see symbols or colors, which, to them, would mean that cancer is present in the abdomen. At times the information can be quite elaborate, with specific details accompanying the initial impression.

The explanation given for the claimed effectiveness of the intuitive process resembles the theory behind radiesthesia. Intuitives or psychic

> Sometimes the practitioners of these methods seem to be guessing. Yet there are some who consistently get accurate results that are verified by conventional diagnostic means.

workers usually claim that the patient's body and mind send out some sort of signal that the intuitive can receive through his or her unconscious mind.

The information that self-proclaimed psychics, sensitives, and intuitives provide, however, is often too vague to be useful. But the stars of the intuitive technique, adherents report, consistently get 75 to 85 percent or greater accuracy in reporting specific personality traits and medical details of physical illnesses. This information is reportedly not the least bit vague, but indicates exactly which organ or part of the body is diseased, and the specific nature of that illness, whether it be malignant, infectious, or allergic.

Few clear patterns
Venturing into the practices of alternative diagnosis is confusing and challenging at best. The spectrum of theories, techniques, and results leaves few clear patterns to study. Sometimes the practitioners of these methods seem to be guessing. Yet there appear to be a few who consistently produce accurate results that may then be verified by conventional techniques of diagnosis.

One significant study of alternative diagnostic practices was conducted by Dr. C. Norman Shealy and reported in his book *Occult Medicine Can Save Your Life* (1985). He began with 25 patients that he had thoroughly evaluated. The only thing these patients had in common was chronic pain in some area of their body. The intuitives to be tested were given only a photograph, and the name and age of the patient.

Not accurate enough
The test for the diagnosticians was to find the area of pain and provide any other useful information. A number of intuitives provided poor results, but 3 out of the 25 were reportedly 70 to 75 percent accurate. Dr. Shealy gave this same test to a psychologist who had no known intuitive abilities: he was only 5 percent accurate. An astrologer and a handwriting expert were also asked to determine the site of physical pain; they were supposedly accurate only 25 to 30 percent of the time.

Do alternative methods of diagnosis work? The only answer that can safely be given is: possibly. Success appears to depend on the skill of the alternative practitioner. However, most doctors do advise that such methods should not be used for primary diagnosis and especially not as a substitute for modern diagnostic techniques.

DEAD ACCURATE
In his book, *Fringe Medicine* (1964), Brian Inglis relates an anecdote that sheds some light on the failures of radionics. It concerns Dr. Aubrey Westlake, who conducted research into the subject for his book *The Pattern of Health* (1961). A chronically ill patient known to Dr. Westlake sent off a blood specimen for analysis by radionics. The radionics operator sent back his first diagnostic report: it stated that there was "an improvement in the patient's condition." Unfortunately, however, the patient had actually died in the interim.

The etheric body
Dr. Westlake asked the operator how he had managed readings on a dead patient, and received an unembarrassed reply. The operator said that radionics "deals with a body other than the physical: the etheric, or astral — and in that case death would have no effect on the readings except that one might find some improvement."

Therapeutic touch
Dolores Krieger demonstrates the technique known as therapeutic touch; despite its name, she passes her hands over the body without touching it.

KIRLIAN PHOTOGRAPHY

Few people claim to be able to see auras with the naked eye. However, there is a technique that produces a photographic image of the electromagnetic field that surrounds all living things.

*I*N 1939 IN THE CITY OF KRASNODAR, southern Russia, an electrician named Semyon Davidovich Kirlian was visiting a medical research institute to collect electrical equipment for repair. On his way through the hospital, he happened to see a demonstration of electrotherapy. When he saw flashes of light spark between the glass-plated electrodes and the patient's fingers, his curiosity was aroused. He decided to try and photograph what he had seen.

Kirlian found that by placing his hand on a sheet of light-sensitive paper on top of a metal plate through which a high-voltage current was passed, he was apparently able to capture on film the electromagnetic energy that was discharged from his hand. On developing the photograph, he was left with a strange luminescent imprint of his hand in which the fingers appeared as if fringed with streaks of light.

Hands-on diagnosis

Kirlian and his wife, Valentina, set up a laboratory to research this phenomenon. The Kirlians believed their electromagnetic photographs could be used for diagnosis of illness. When the Kirlians demonstrated their research at a Moscow scientific conference, the photographs of Semyon's hands displayed a marked difference from those of his wife. Semyon's hands showed up as indistinct and blurred with a cloudy outline, whereas Valentina's hands were clear with a

Kirlian fingertip
This Kirlian effect was created when a high-voltage electrical current flowed through an insulated electrode. The corona of energy that was generated was recorded on color film.

Healing touch
This Kirlian photograph is of a healer's hand while at work. The clearly defined coronas of discharge around the fingertips and the yellow area in the center of the palm are sometimes seen in healers' hands.

> **Kirlian photographers believe it is possible to tell a person's state of health from the color and pattern of the photograph.**

well-defined outline. Hours later Semyon fell sick with a bout of influenza. The Kirlians believed that the indistinct outline was a sign of his oncoming illness.

Kirlian photographers believe it is possible to tell a person's state of health from the color and pattern of the photograph. If the outline of a hand is jagged or indistinct, this indicates that the subject is ill or upset. If the palm photograph is even and clearly outlined, then the subject is a well-balanced and healthy individual.

A reliable tool?

Kirlian photographs have been used in medical research. Doctors Michael Shacter and David Sheinkin of Pomona, New York, took Kirlian handprints of schizophrenics before and after treatment. Before treatment there was apparently no clearly defined corona around the fingertips, as is seen in a healthy patient. After treatment the gaps in the corona appeared to have closed.

The reliability of Kirlian photographs as a means of diagnosis of physical and psychological disorders is not without problems for many members of the scientific

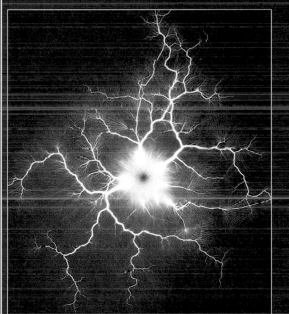

Ball of light
Startling visual effects can be achieved with Kirlian photographs of non-organic subjects. This lightning effect has been created by dropping a steel ball into a high-energy electrical field.

Leaf aura
This Kirlian photograph records the coronal discharge, or energy, given off by a maple leaf when exposed to a high-energy electrical field.

establishment. Professor Arthur Ellison of City University, London, has found that certain environmental factors — such as temperature, humidity, and pressure of the hand on the photographic paper — produce changes in the photograph. He also found that sweat could influence the result, as could the subject's intake of alcohol, tobacco, or drugs.

However, Thelma Moss of the School of Medicine at UCLA, one of the leading original American researchers into Kirlian photography, argued that even if the coloring and luminescence of the palm print changes under certain conditions, then this in itself is worthy of further research. Her work established that when a subject is relaxed, the corona around the fingertips is more colorful than in a tense or excitable subject.

CHAPTER FIVE

BODY WORK

Some therapies concentrate on the body to achieve their special effects. Exercises, massage, and careful diet management, some claim, can promote health in mind, body, and spirit.

The last century has seen the dramatic proliferation of a wide range of therapies designed to enhance emotional and spiritual well-being by making the body healthier. For the most part, these techniques have been pioneered by people seeking to emphasize crucial connections between mind and body, and between Western medicine and psychoanalysis.

Many of these holistic pioneers knew that such links had been made in the East. Disciplines like yoga and tai chi chuan coordinate mind, body, and spirit, and aspects of these ancient sciences form a vital part of the new body-mind therapies.

The Alexander technique

One of the first theorists to explore this territory was an Australian actor named Frederick Matthias Alexander (1869–1955). When, during rehearsals, he became hoarse and lost his voice, he visited various doctors. To his dismay, he found that all they had to offer were ineffectual throat sprays.

Alexander began to examine himself in a mirror and noticed that, when he recited his lines, he let his head sag, thus depressing his larynx. When he kept his neck straight and his head erect, the problem disappeared. He came to believe that better posture resulted in greater ease, more physical freedom, and increased efficiency of movement. He abandoned his acting career to develop and practice his new therapy, which he called the Alexander technique.

The technique involves a form of body education; and so practitioners are called teachers, and their clients, pupils. By guiding and positioning pupils' bodies with their hands, teachers demonstrate the natural relationship of head, neck, and spine, and reeducate the body so that it can be used effectively. It is hard to break old, bad body habits, adherents warn, especially those that are so ingrained that they feel right.

The Alexander technique is often utilized by musicians, actors, singers, and dancers, and by those who suffer from problems that are partially linked to either body misalignment or stress and tension, such as migraine, headache, and asthma. In addition to dealing with specific problems, practitioners believe that the technique can be valuable as a preventive measure against organic and structural ailments.

The Feldenkrais method

About the same time the Alexander technique was being developed, Russian-born research physicist Moshe Feldenkrais was working thousands of miles away in what is now Israel, on a

Moshe Feldenkrais

> He believed that mental attitudes could be changed by altering negative physical patterns: "The only thing permanent about your behavior patterns," he said "is your belief that they are so."

similar system of body retraining to improve posture and general health. As well as being a scientist, Feldenkrais was one of the first non-Japanese judo black belts and an avid soccer player. It was the recurrence of an old knee injury that inspired him to examine the mechanics of human movement and its relationship to behavior and learning.

Personality in motion

His theory was that each person has a unique set of unconscious movements that are a physical expression of his or her personality. Many of these movements reflect old habits and characteristics that have become lodged, permanently and certainly destructively, in the body and thus in the personality. He believed that mental attitudes could be changed by altering negative physical patterns: "The only thing permanent about your behavior patterns," he said, "is your belief that they are so."

There are two kinds of training in the Feldenkrais method: One, known as Awareness Through Movement, involves group work and takes the form of simple gentle exercises, done mostly lying on the floor. These exercises offer the brain better and healthier ways to use the body. The second method of teaching is called Functional Integration; this is an individual, hands-on approach particularly suited to those in pain, or with specific disabilities.

The Trager system

Milton Trager (born in 1908) is a retired American physician now living in southern California, who developed a

♦ PAGE 110

STAGECRAFT

F. M. Alexander first retrained his own body to achieve greater health, then taught his technique to others.

FREDERICK MATTHIAS ALEXANDER, the founder of the Alexander technique, was born on a farm in Tasmania, Australia, in 1869. Usually called F. M. by his parents, and later his friends, he was the eldest of eight children, and from an early age was both difficult and sickly. After the age of nine, he had little formal education, and little if any exposure to the theater, yet he developed a strong interest in acting, particularly in declaiming Shakespeare.

Early ambitions

His first ambition was to become a teacher, but his family could not afford to train him. When he was 16, he went to work in a tin mine. After three years, he had earned enough to finance a stay in Melbourne, where he began to give Shakespeare recitals. These soon attracted large audiences. But then he developed serious problems with his voice, and it was these that he cured by developing techniques to improve his posture. This inspired him to formalize his system of posture and movement enhancement.

The success of Alexander and his technique led other actors to consult him. Soon he was treating the general public as well. In time, he gave up performing altogether to concentrate on treating patients. He made further use of his skills as director of the Sydney Dramatic and Operatic Conservatorium.

Successful treatments

In 1904, at the age of 34, he moved to London, where he treated such famous actors as Sir Henry Irving, Herbert Beerbohm Tree, and Lily Langtry, and the writers Aldous Huxley and George Bernard Shaw. Among the teachers he trained was his younger brother Albert, who, for a time, established a successful practice in New York.

To explain and disseminate his ideas, Alexander produced several books, including his most famous, *The Use of Self* (1932).

Alexander spent part of the Second World War in the United States, but returned to England in 1943. Even in his seventies, he continued to teach for up to 16 hours each day, demonstrating a remarkable level of energy, one that he credited to the lifelong utilization of his ideas. When he was 79, he had a slight stroke, but recovered completely, and continued to teach until his death at the age of 86.

Frederick Matthias Alexander

The spinal column
The Alexander technique is based on the idea that correct posture, including a straight back, will result in better general health and give relief from a variety of illnesses. Students of the technique learn to overcome poor posture, so that they stand and move correctly.

system of gentle, non-intrusive movements when he was 18. An amateur boxer, Trager was giving his manager a massage when he discovered that squeezing, thumping, and rubbing are not necessarily the best ways to loosen and relax muscles. In fact, such actions can make them tighter.

By substituting shaking or rocking, or by using gentle, rhythmic motions, Trager found that he could release built-up tension, and encourage relaxation, and thus increase physical mobility and improve mental clarity.

Dr. Milton Trager

Rolfing

Dr. Ida Rolf (1896–1979) graduated with a Ph.D. in biological chemistry from Columbia University, and then went to work at Rockefeller University. During the 1930's Rolf turned her attention to the structure and functioning of the body and eventually founded a system of structural integration now known as Rolfing.

Like Feldenkrais, Dr. Rolf believed that the body reflects mental and emotional attitudes, which in turn are formed by the stresses and strains of life. She perceived the human body as a pile of building blocks stacked one above the other, with the spinal column running down the center. Her theory was that, from early life onward, these stresses and strains shift the blocks out of alignment. Once a shift has begun, gravity pulls the blocks farther off center and the muscles then attempt to compensate for the misalignment, which leads to structural disintegration.

To deal with this, Rolfing makes use of deep massage and manipulation. This is intended to restore the body to its normal, smoothly integrated position and release it from "body armoring," which is produced by tension and rigidity in both the muscles and the connective tissues.

Several people who were once affiliated with Dr. Rolf later broke away to develop their own systems of therapy, which are related to Rolfing, but not approved by the Rolf Institute. One of the best known of these systems is called Hellerwork, after its inventor, Joseph Heller, a former president of the Rolf Institute.

Hellerwork comprises three phases: body work, a form of manipulative therapy; movement education, which trains the patient to move in such a way that stress is reduced; and dialogue, in which patient and practitioner discuss how the mind and emotions affect the overall state of the body.

Dr. Ida Rolf

> She saw the human body as a pile of building blocks stacked one above the other, with the spinal column running down the center.

FREEING THE LIFE FORCE

Among the many holistic therapies, there are two, naturopathy and polarity therapy, that are based on the same premise: If the body is provided with inner cleanliness, a nutritious diet, appropriate exercise, and a positive mental outlook, it will sustain the highest possible degree of health.

NATUROPATHY AND POLARITY THERAPY are based on the theory that the body can and should heal itself. Both require from their practitioners a strong commitment to positive change and a willingness to take responsibility for their own health.

Naturopathy

One of the most ancient of all therapy systems is naturopathy. It has among its supporters the Greek physician Hippocrates who, about 400 B.C., referred to the "healing power of nature." He laid down guidelines for good health: sufficient rest and exercise, adequate nourishment, and emotional stability.

The basis of naturopathy is that the body always acts in its own best interests. Thus a symptom, however painful it may be, is the body's way of drawing attention to, and dealing with, a problem, and thus should not be suppressed unless absolutely necessary. This is particularly true in the case of fever, which Hippocrates said is the root of healing. "Give me a fever and I will cure my patient." Instead of treating the symptom, the practitioner examines the patient as a whole in order to find the underlying cause of the disease and restore normal function, thus allowing the body to heal itself.

To do this, the naturopath may use one or a number of reportedly holistic treatments that seem appropriate: chiropractic, acupuncture, shiatsu, massage, hydrotherapy, counseling, homeopathy, herbalism, or relaxation techniques. Many naturopaths are qualified practitioners in several of these disciplines.

Fasting is often recommended to begin, but the strictness of the diet is determined by the patient's reserves of vital energy and his or her ability to respond to the treatment. A short period of fasting is believed to release reserves of energy rather than to deplete the body's supply of energy.

Polarity therapy

Developed by Austrian osteopath, chiropractor, and naturopath, Dr. Randolph Stone (1890–1981), polarity therapy blends these techniques with those of Eastern medicine, which includes the idea that the body's energy flows between a positive and a negative pole, with a neutral point in the middle. This flow is affected by the five elements, each of which has an energy center in the body. Polarity therapy tries to balance the energy flow and the energy centers in several ways.

In therapeutic touch the practitioner places his or her hands on the patient's body to set up a field between positive and negative poles. Then, either soothing, balancing, "neutral" pressure, is applied, or some form of manipulation is undertaken: "positive" manipulation to create movement of energy, or "negative" manipulation to disperse blockages.

Negative eating patterns

The therapist may also try to correct negative eating patterns the patients may have, and help them purify their bodies of toxins. One method adherents advocate is the "liver flush," a mixture of lemon juice, olive oil, garlic, and ginger. Polarity yoga, a system of exercises designed to reduce blockages and tension, may also help. Though generally non-injurious, and sometimes helpful, such techniques should not replace traditional medical practice when serious medical problems are involved.

Cosmic duality
The two sides of human nature, often represented as male and female, were linked to mystical theories about the universe as shown by the magical symbols in the illustration.

THE MAGIC TOUCH

Chiropractic, acupressure, and shiatsu are all manipulative therapies. Proponents claim that they may be able to correct spinal alignment, enhance well-being, and even ease certain illnesses.

ONE OF THE MOST PROFOUND ways in which modern medicine differs from ancient healing is the lessening of physical contact between today's doctors and their patients. Several complementary therapies, however, seek to enhance healing — either to the whole person, or to specific parts of the body — by applying direct manual pressure to muscles, ligaments, tendons, or joints. These are usually called manipulative therapies. Often, as in earlier times, they rely on the sensitivity of the therapist's hands, and this sensitivity, although clearly natural to some degree, is developed through experience and formal training.

In theory, such therapies operate on a holistic level, using their respective techniques in an attempt to cure both injuries and chronic conditions, and to give the patient an increased sense of well-being. In practice, however, some of the best-known therapies, particularly chiropractic and osteopathy, are frequently employed to treat specific musculoskeletal complaints such as back pain and joint stiffness.

In the swing
An osteopath treats a young girl by holding her head still and swinging her between his hands like a pendulum.

Osteopathy

Originally a complementary therapy — and still practiced as such in many countries around the world — osteopathy has now been accepted in the United States as part of orthodox medicine. Its practitioners are fully qualified doctors, who have specialized in osteopathy during their medical training. They therefore can prescribe drugs and administer chemotherapeutic injections.

Osteopathy was developed in 1874 by a doctor from Virginia named Andrew Taylor Still. Still was inspired to develop a new form of medicine because of the death of three of his children from viral meningitis. Having had five years' training as an engineer, Still came to believe that all disease could

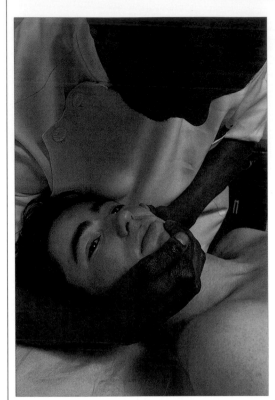

Osteopathic manipulation
An osteopath holds his patient in order to manipulate the cervical (neck) region.

Axis vertebra
The second vertebra below the skull; it allows side-to-side movement of the head.

Atlas vertebra
The first vertebra, it allows the head to nod.

be cured by mechanical adjustments of the body. He coined the word *osteopathy* to describe the new technique by combining two Greek words, *osteos* (bone) and *pathos* (disease).

One of Still's guiding principles was that disease develops when circulation is impeded in any way, because the substances that maintain immunity are manufactured and transported by the blood. His theory was that structural disturbances (which he called "osteopathic lesions"), especially those affecting the spine, blocked the circulation of blood throughout the body and were therefore responsible for disease of every kind.

Still's theory of lesions, however, was abandoned by osteopaths in 1948. Today they no longer claim that their techniques are a complete healing system. They do, however, continue to rely on Still's detailed study of anatomy and the skills he developed as a result. These have led to an extremely effective form of treatment for a wide range of musculo-skeletal complaints.

Modern osteopathic training concentrates both on manipulation skills, which tend to entail leverage rather than direct thrusting actions, and soft-tissue massage, which is designed to release tension and muscle spasm around affected joints, and increase blood circulation in muscles and ligaments. When osteopaths see a new patient for the first time, they take a

Chiropractic technique
A chiropractor in Mali uses the technique to manipulate a client's back.

detailed medical history, then make a thorough physical examination of joints and muscles in order to establish an appropriate course of treatment.

Chiropractic

Chiropractic (from the Greek words *cheiro* and *praktikos*, meaning manual practice) is another widely recognized manipulative therapy. It was the creation of a medically untrained Canadian-born healer, Daniel David Palmer (1845–1913).

> **Palmer thought that spinal displacement led to disease and pain by causing a disturbance not of the circulation, but of the central nervous system.**

Always interested in anatomy in general, and the workings of the spine in particular, Palmer practiced several types of hand healing in towns up and down the Mississippi. He studied Andrew Taylor Still's theories before settling in Iowa and, in 1885, developing his own technique of spinal adjustment.

He first became intrigued by the possibilities of such a technique when he was reportedly successful in healing a man named Harvey Lillard, the caretaker

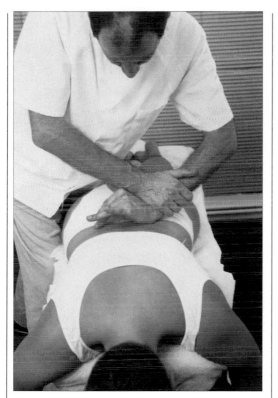

Adjusting the spinal column
A chiropractor adjusts a lumbar vertebra, trying to correct a misalignment with a thrust using between 7 and 14 pounds of pressure.

of a building where Palmer was employed. Lillard had lost his hearing 17 years earlier, after straining his back. At the time, he had experienced considerable pain, and felt something "go." On examining him, Palmer discovered a painful and prominently displaced vertebra, which he pushed forcefully back into position. Almost immediately, Lillard is said to have experienced an improvement in his hearing. Additional treatments apparently restored it.

Further spinal examinations on other patients led Daniel David Palmer to believe that correcting displaced vertebrae (which he called subluxations) frequently relieved complaints in other parts of the body.

Recognized technique

Chiropractic is accepted in every state, as well as in Canada, Britain, Australia, New Zealand, and many European countries. Chiropractors study for four years, covering not only chiropractic, but also subjects such as anatomy, physiology, chemistry, microbiology, and

pathology, with particular emphasis on the study of radiology and physics.

Both Still and Palmer believed that the spine held the key to the body's ills, but Palmer thought that spinal displacement led to disease and pain by causing a disturbance not of the circulation, but of the central nervous system. In modern practice, chiropractors approach patients in much the same way as osteopaths, by taking a complete medical history, then doing a physical examination.

The systems differ in the most general terms, however, in that chiropractors manipulate the joints using direct thrusts rather than leverage. They also tend to concentrate less on the body's soft tissues than osteopaths.

Acupressure

Acupressure, said to be the forerunner of acupuncture, is Chinese acupuncture without the use of needles. The technique was later adopted in Japan, where it is known as shiatsu. The body's acupressure points are massaged to stimulate and balance the flow of energy through the body. The vital life energy that runs through these acupressure points is known as chi.

A study at the Department of Anaesthetics at Belfast University has shown that acupressure can be of use in combating nausea, produced by seasickness for example, by wearing a band on the arm near the wrist. It exerts pressure on a specific point on the arm called Pericardium 6, which is about two inches above the wrist joint.

Shiatsu

Increasingly popular in the West, shiatsu is an ancient Japanese form of acupressure massage in which particular points on the body (called *tsubos*) are manipulated to ease pain and tension, correct faulty circulation, improve metabolism, and treat a wide variety of diseases such as high blood pressure, arthritis and rheumatism, and diabetes. Practiced widely in Japan, shiatsu in its present form is only about 80 years old. The basic technique has, however, been used in Japan since Chinese medicine

Thoracic vertebra
The 12 thoracic vertebrae are located in the chest; they move slightly every time a breath is taken.

Cervical vertebra
One of seven vertebrae in the neck; together they allow the head to turn.

THE SPINE

Both osteopaths and chiropractors concentrate on the spine, believing that it influences the health of the whole body.

It is indisputable that the spine plays a vital role within the body, conveying nerve impulses from the brain to the limbs and trunk. If the spinal cord is severed, paralysis results below the point at which the damage occurs.

The back bone is designed to protect the fragile spinal cord. It consists of the vertebrae, a row of 24 bones separated by fleshy pads called discs, and the spinal cord itself. The spinal cord is a thick bundle of nerve fibers that connects the brain to the rest of the body.

(on which the technique is based) was introduced about a thousand years ago. Modern shiatsu was developed early in the 20th century by Tokujiro Namikoshi, whose work in formalizing the therapy's techniques led to its official recognition by the Japanese Ministry of Health and Welfare. Although the word "shiatsu" is translated as "finger pressure," the palm and heel of the hands, and even the knuckles, elbows, knees, and feet are employed to provide the required pressure in the form of stroking, rubbing, kneading, tapping, shaking and stretching, as well as pressing. No equipment or tools of any kind are used. The treatment can be given anywhere, and the only special requirement is that the patient wear loose clothing. Although professional practitioners undergo extensive training, shiatsu is also used as a home remedy in Japan. It is practiced by family members for everyday complaints, such as headaches and stress.

Unblocking energy channels

According to Takujiro Namikoshi: "Shiatsu strives first of all to prevent illness and, by calling forth innate self-curative powers, to develop bodies capable of resisting sickness." These powers come from the *chi*, which, according to Oriental medicine, flows through energy channels in the body

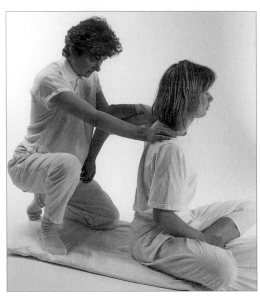

Under pressure
A shiatsu practitioner exerts pressure on a patient's shoulder. This part of the body is thought to correspond to the intestines and is often tense.

which are known as meridians. (These channels are the same as those that are treated in acupuncture.)

Shiatsu aims to balance energy in the body by working on the meridians, each of which is associated with the function of a different organ. In order to balance the chi running through that meridian, the practitioner presses on the relevant *tsubos*. If it feels hollow, the chi is weak, and the meridian is "tonified" to add more; if the *tsubos* feels hard, this means there is excessive chi, and it is dispersed.

Apart from touch, shiatsu practitioners use a wide variety of other diagnostic techniques. They observe the skin color, particularly on the face and along the meridian lines; they examine the tongue; they listen to the sound of the patient's voice; and they may even take his or her pulse. In fact, this involves taking 12 pulses, six in each wrist, related to the 12 meridians. Practitioners also attempt to sense what is occurring in the patient's *hara* (energy center), which is situated just below the navel and is thought to be the source of chi.

Lumbar vertebra

Lumbar vertebra
(viewed from above)
The five lumbar vertebrae in the lower back support the weight of the upper body. These vertebrae are therefore under the greatest strain. Not surprisingly, the lumbar region is the area in which back pain is most common.

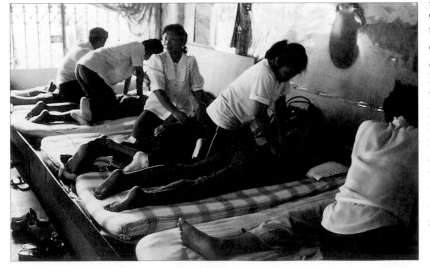

Acupressure
In the Union of Myanmar (formerly Burma) acupressure is even performed in the temples, as here at the temple complex of the Reclining Buddha.

A HEAD START ON HEALTH

At the end of the 19th century, William Garner Sutherland, a pupil of Andrew Taylor Still, created the discipline known as cranial osteopathy, in which the bones of the skull are delicately manipulated in an attempt to correct damage or misalignment.

ALTHOUGH ORTHODOX MEDICINE held that the bones of the human skull fuse together by the age of 30, William Garner Sutherland reportedly found while studying osteopathy that these bones can in fact be manipulated to make minute movements throughout life. He believed that this motion had an effect on all the associated organs and tissues of the head and spinal column.

Preventing shocks to the system

Furthermore, Sutherland maintained that the brain and central nervous system expand and contract with a rhythmical pulse that is independent of the heart or breathing rate, and can be felt in all body tissues, but most particularly in the skull and pelvic regions. His theory was that this rhythmical pulse, which he called the primary respiratory mechanism, pumps cerebro-spinal fluid up and down the spine and around the brain, where it absorbs shocks and provides nourishment for the central nervous system.

If the body suffers any physical shock, for example from a blow to the head or a car accident, the resulting stresses can lay dormant for years in the connective tissues, interfering with this mechanism and causing pain and discomfort. Other factors that

> **Practitioners claim that cranial osteopathy has a profound effect on health and is helpful in dealing with a wide range of conditions.**

are claimed to affect the cranial pulse are stress, which makes the muscles tense, and toxins (present in many foods and in polluted air). A cranial osteopath supposedly detects congestion and stress by monitoring the strength and regularity of this pulse, then eases it by using gentle pressure on various parts of the body, especially the head and the base of the neck.

Although the treatment is very delicate, practitioners claim that cranial osteopathy has a profound effect on health and is helpful in dealing with a wide range of conditions, such as migraine and other headaches, injuries, and postural and degenerative conditions.

Being treated is said to be very relaxing. Practitioners claim it is useful for babies and children with problems that may have been caused by a difficult birth, such as epilepsy or cerebral palsy, and also for autistic children.

But whatever the claims of the cranial osteopaths themselves, this specialty has not found favor with conventionally trained physicians. Yet many doctors would agree that while it has no medical or scientific basis, it does not appear to be harmful as long as it does not prevent or delay patients from seeking trained medical advice in the case of serious ailments or injuries.

How the skull is formed
The skull is made up of eight separate bones. At birth, the fontanelles, six membranes between the bones of the skull, are not hardened. This allows the baby's head to pass more easily through the birth canal. In newborn infants, the largest of these fontanelles can be seen at the top of skull. As the child grows, the skull hardens and the bones move together. Even in the skull of an adult, the joints between the bones, which are known as sutures, are visible as wavy lines.

Adult skull

Baby skull

YOU ARE WHAT YOU EAT

Most doctors now believe that diet and health are closely linked and that eating a healthy diet can help prevent illnesses such as heart disease. Some healers go further and make controversial claims that special diets may be able to cure such life-threatening diseases as cancer.

A BALANCED APPROACH

Macrobiotics is based on the ancient Eastern classifications of yin and yang, and the importance of balance between them. It is an approach to nutrition rather than a specific diet.

In dietary terms, yin foods are those that thrive in hot climates, have a high percentage of water, grow high above the ground, and take the form of fruits or leaves. Yang foods are native to cold climates, fairly dry, often grown below ground, and come from the plant's stems, roots, or seeds.

Eating the macrobiotic way

One of the primary principles of macrobiotics is that eating indigenous vegetables in season will maintain the perfect yin − yang balance naturally. When they are available, legumes like peas and beans are considered particularly beneficial. Whole grains are the other staple of the macrobiotic diet. Enthusiasts believe they should be consumed at every meal and constitute half, or more, of every day's normal food intake.

An ideal diet will also include fruit occasionally, fish two or three times per week, and even meat from time to time. A few roasted seeds or nuts may also be eaten, as well as a little sesame, corn, or other natural oil.

Expert opinion

This regime, however, is not recommended by doctors and nutritionists, because it is likely to be deficient in vitamins and minerals. If followed in extreme form, where only brown rice is eaten, it can lead to malnutrition and anemia. Some proponents of the diet claim that it can cure cancer. In fact, it can lower the body's resistance to the illness.

AS INCREASED PROSPERITY and advances in food technology lower the incidence of illness caused by poor nutrition, more and more lives are being claimed by conditions related to dietary excess, such as coronary artery disease, strokes, high blood pressure, diabetes, and some cancers.

Most people are aware that a wholesome diet should be low in fat, salt, sugar, and alcohol, and should contain a high proportion of whole grains and fresh fruit and vegetables. The health of most people who eat a traditional Western diet high in fat and refined foods would benefit from not overeating or even by simply avoiding fatty fried foods and sugary cakes and cookies.

Change for the better

The first step to healthier eating is to ensure that your diet contains a high proportion of fresh, low-fat foods. Plant foods in peak condition, ripe, grown in fertile soil, and unprocessed are best — to obtain the most from them, it is best to eat them as close to their natural state as possible, preferably raw or lightly cooked. Bread and pasta made with wholemeal flour, and brown (unpolished) rice are more healthful than white rice and unbleached white flour. This is because the brown hulls of rice and wheat, which are removed during processing, are not only rich in vitamins but are also a good source of fiber.

The best fruits and vegetables are those that are local and seasonal. These are likely to retain more of their vitamins than hothouse varieties, or exotic specimens that have been imported from faraway places. Keep in mind, however, that produce frozen when it is picked often contains more nutritional value than its "fresh" equivalent, which may have spent several days on a supermarket shelf.

Foods to avoid

Avoid foods that are high in salt and saturated fat, such as potato or corn chips; also avoid sweet carbonated drinks, candy, and packaged bread, cakes, and cookies that contain high levels of artificial coloring, flavoring, and preservatives. Large quantities of red meat, such as

Most people are aware that a wholesome diet should be low in fat, salt, sugar, and alcohol, and should contain a high proportion of whole grains and fresh fruit and vegetables.

> As well as encouraging a high level of general health, individual foods may be used, in theory at least, to treat some illnesses and chronic conditions.

beef, are believed by some to be difficult to digest. Research by the pressure group Center for Science in the Public Interest has also shown that beef may contain unacceptable amounts of chemicals deposited in the animal by growth hormones, medicines, and treated feed.

Eating for energy

Many experts also believe that the time at which we eat our meals is almost as vital as what we eat. In her book *Let's Eat Right to Keep Fit*, author and nutritionist Adele Davis maintained that a protein-rich breakfast is essential not only for establishing the healthy blood sugar level and rate of metabolism necessary for energy, concentration, and general well-being, but also for maintaining these levels throughout the day.

Eating the heaviest meal of the day late in the evening and then going without breakfast can result in a feeling of lethargy. Those who follow this eating pattern may find that they operate at half speed throughout the day, arriving home listless and hungry and ready to consume another large meal, thus perpetuating a potentially damaging dietary pattern.

Medicinal meals

As well as encouraging a high level of general health, individual foods may be used, in theory at least, to treat some illnesses and chronic conditions. This is because some contain substances that may be helpful, without having side effects. Pineapples, figs, and artichokes, for example, contain an enzyme that aids digestion, while onions, apples, oats, beans, and garlic, may help reduce the level of cholesterol in the blood significantly.

Fresh is best
Most of the benefits of garlic, many experts believe, are lost when it is made into pills or extracts. Fresh garlic is said to be more effective in lowering blood pressure.

▶ PAGE 122

PLANT FOOD

Although some vegetarians choose it for moral, economic, or religious reasons, a vegetarian diet has a great deal to recommend it on the basis of health alone. In the West, for example, vegetarians have a lower incidence of heart disease, diabetes, and certain types of cancer than people who eat meat. Because of these health benefits, the American Dietetic Association has declared that vegetarian diets are "healthful and nutritionally adequate when properly planned."

Most modern vegetarians are lacto-ovo vegetarians, which means they also eat eggs and dairy products. A few, however, are vegans — that is, they do not eat any animal products at all.

Their diets include only plant foods such as cereals, nuts, legumes, fruit and vegetables, and seed and vegetable oils. Milk and cheese substitutes are made from soya beans. Semivegetarians choose to eat only small amounts of white meat like fish and poultry, but not red meat such as beef, pork, or lamb. This type of diet is low in fat and confers most of the health benefits of a vegetarian diet.

Essential nutrients

If properly planned, a vegetarian diet need not be lacking in essential nutrients. Care must be taken, however, to get enough protein, since vegetable sources of protein, such as grains and legumes, do not contain all the essential amino acids. It is possible to get a complete supply of amino acids, but only by carefully combining protein sources such as rice and beans. To avoid nutrient deficiencies, vegetarians should eat a wide range of foods.

The staff of life
A simple diet of breads, beans, other legumes, fruit, and vegetables may be healthier than one including meat.

ALLERGIC TO THE 20TH CENTURY

In the modern world we are in daily contact with thousands of different chemicals and pollutants. They surround us in our homes and workplaces and can be found in the air, water, and food. Severe problems arise when people become allergic to these substances.

IN THE SAME WAY THAT SOME PEOPLE are allergic to certain foods, others have a violent physical reaction to some common environmental chemicals. In addition to causing reactions in sensitive individuals, these everyday substances may be responsible for precipitating a wide range of symptoms, such as fatigue, headaches, skin irritations, arthritis, and digestive problems.

Chemical culprits

In most cases, the offending chemicals are not suspect because their use is widespread. Obvious culprits are some pesticides and fertilizers used in growing crops, and the artificial colorings, flavorings, and preservatives often employed in the processing of food and beverages. Serious problems can also be triggered by noncomestible chemicals, however, and these may

> At their worst, these allergies may become so numerous and acute in a person that he or she will be unable to function normally and may be forced to live in isolation.

include the perfumes in cosmetics and toiletries, the formaldehyde in many home furnishing materials and adhesives, the polyurethane foam in upholstered seating, the synthetic fibers in clothing, and the chlorine in tap water. Some people even react to the chemicals in plastic or treated metal food containers.

Heightened sensitivity

Even if one of these substances does not trigger a reaction right away, sensitivity may build up over a long period, or the effects may be cumulative. In both cases, symptoms may not appear until some time after first exposure to the particular environmental chemicals. Similarly, some chemicals, although they may not produce a reaction by themselves, interact, producing what is called a synergistic reaction.

At their worst, these allergies may become so numerous and acute in a person that he or she will be unable to function normally and may be forced to live in isolation. Some people who suffer in this way have to

live in a controlled, sterile environment, completely isolated from the modern world.

For sufferers, the situation is as difficult as it is dangerous: The U.S. alone produces over 500 billion

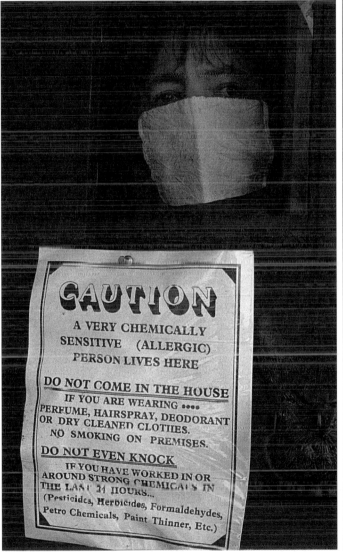

A sterile environment
Some unfortunate individuals have acute reactions to pollutants in the air or to common household chemicals and are forced to live in protected environments, isolated from the modern world.

pounds of chemicals every year, and the computer register of the Chemical Abstract Service lists over 4 million different types of chemical substances, 33,000 of which are currently in common use.

Fruits and cheeses

WINNING COMBINATIONS
There are a number of diets based on the principle of food combining, but the best known is the Hay diet (also known as Fundamental Eating), formulated by William Howard Hay in the 1930's and described in his book *Health via Food.*

Hay believed that because the human digestive system is not designed to process concentrated proteins and starches simultaneously, these foods should never be eaten at the same meal. In practice, this means avoiding many traditional combinations such as meat and potatoes, spaghetti and meatballs, and most sandwiches.

The three food groups
In working out his eating plan, Hay divided food into three main categories: protein foods, starch foods, and neutral foods, which can be combined with those from either of the other two groups. According to this system, protein foods include not only obvious things like meat, fish, eggs, and cheese, but also most fruits and pulses. The starch group consists of bread, potatoes, grains, and some fruits like bananas, ripe pears, and very sweet grapes. Apart from potatoes, most vegetables are neutral, as are nuts, butter and oils, seeds, cream, and honey.

Supporters of this system believe that combining foods in the wrong way leads not only to digestive problems, but to a wide range of serious illnesses.

Garlic is believed to be a particularly potent food. If eaten in sufficient quantities, it has a beneficial effect on cholesterol, and it has reportedly been shown to lower blood pressure and act as an anticoagulant. However, large quantities of garlic are likely to cause nausea and bad breath.

Garlic may also help fight infections of many kinds, since it is believed to be antibacterial, antifungal, and antiviral in nature. Honey too has antiseptic properties. It is considered by some to be an effective treatment for several allergies, especially hay fever.

Vitamin A
Lung problems such as respiratory infections and some kinds of cancer are thought by some to respond to the high levels of vitamin A-rich beta carotene in carrots; the vitamin is also thought to help relieve skin and eye problems. High levels of vitamin A should, however, be avoided during pregnancy as they have been linked to birth defects.

You are what you eat
Behavior, as well as physical health, can be affected by the things we eat and drink; the caffeine in tea, coffee, and cola, for instance, is a stimulant. Drinking excessive amounts of these beverages can result in irritability. American nutritionist Alexander Schauss would add unbleached white flour, sugar, and other highly refined foods to the list of those that can disturb behavior. Grapes, wheatgerm, and molasses, on the other hand, are natural substances that are said to have a calming effect.

Can diet cure disease?
Some illnesses, such as diabetes, can clearly be alleviated by following a special diet. Other common complaints, such as feelings of fatigue and lethargy, may be reduced by simply eating a better diet. Certainly good nutrition can improve your quality of life.

Some alternative therapists, however, claim that specific illnesses and conditions can be cured by eating large amounts of certain foods that are thought to heal and avoiding others believed to be harmful. For example, carrot and celery juice are often recommended to fight cancer, whilst smoked foods are considered harmful and should be avoided. Yet such extreme or specific dietary measures are not orthodox medical practice because their effectiveness has never been clearly substantiated by scientific research.

Energy boost
Tokyo businessmen boost their energy levels by drinking concoctions made from ingredients such as ginseng — used in Chinese medicine to counter fatigue.

FIGHTING CANCER

In 1982 the National Cancer Institute published an important report on the relationship between diet and cancer, and strongly recommended a particular way of eating to discourage the onset of the disease.

*I*T IS A SIMPLE MATTTER, according to modern medical wisdom, to reduce your risk of cancer. All you have to do is eat more fresh fruit, vegetables, and whole grains, and cut down on fats, alcohol, and smoked, salt-cured, and pickled foods.

Other foods thought to contain carcinogenic (cancer-producing) agents include rancid fats, oils, and nuts; processed meats; artificial sweeteners; coal-tar colorings; and overheated and re-heated oils. Some molds can also cause cancer. Even if the mold is scraped off, the food will still be unfit to eat, since toxins are able to migrate from the surface of the food.

Danger foods and cancer

In some cases, specific foods seem to be linked with certain types of cancer. A high intake of meat, for example, is associated with cancer of the bowel, pancreas, and prostate. A diet that includes large quantities of smoked foods — such as bacon, other smoked meats and fish, and "char-grilled" steaks — seems to encourage stomach cancer, especially when combined with an excessive intake of salt.

> A high-fiber diet helps to reduce the incidence of some of the cancers associated with the Western way of life.

Conversely, some foods appear to help keep cancer at bay. Extra-virgin olive oil, nuts (especially almonds), whole-grain breads and cereals, wheat germ, and dark green vegetables all contain high levels of vitamin A. In a Finnish study published in the *American Journal of Epidemiology* in 1988, vitamin A was found to lower the risk of smoking-related cancers.

A high-fiber diet helps to reduce the incidence of some of the cancers associated with the Western way of life, including colorectal cancer, breast cancer, prostatic cancer, and endometric cancer. Such cancers are all but unknown among primitive people whose diet is largely made up of high-fiber foods. This may be due to the important role fiber plays in the digestive process, carrying toxins and carcinogens safely out of the body.

The eminent British surgeon and cancer researcher, Dr. Denis Burkitt, is a passionate polemicist on the subject of fiber. He wrote in the *Journal of Nutrition* in 1988: "Ten different countries have now published dietary guidelines for their populations. There is almost total agreement between them. Fiber and starch are protective. Fat, sugar, and salt are causative."

Reaching for the heights
Alternative treatments for cancer have included special diets, exercise, relaxation, and confidence-building. Here Japanese cancer patients climb Mont Blanc to boost their self-belief.

HERBAL CURES

The practice of herbalism — the preparation of the seeds, stems, roots, and leaves of plants for use as medicines and ointments — has seen a dramatic revival in recent years.

THE RECORDS OF MANY ANCIENT CIVILIZATIONS refer to the art of herbalism. Herbal cures are listed in the works of the Chinese emperor Shen Nung, for example, which date back to 3000 B.C. From humankind's earliest history right up until the 17th century, medicines were made almost exclusively from plants and plant extracts. But the 17th century saw the introduction of mineral and chemical ingredients. Although many important medicines currently in use are still plant based, conventional medicine is highly selective in its use of plant extracts in modern drugs, and utilizes only the active plant ingredient in the manufacturing process.

By contrast, herbalists advocate the use of remedies made exclusively from plants. And there has recently been a resurgence of interest in traditional herbalism. By the 1990's sales of herbal products, which had been virtually nonexistent only a decade before, represented a multi-million-dollar industry.

Sassafras leaves

Aromatic leaves
The sassafras, also known as the ague tree, is an aromatic-leafed north American tree. The bark of the root in particular is used in a number of herbal medicines and in herbal tea.

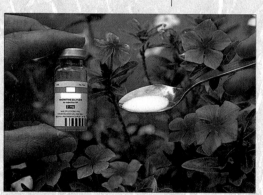

Cancer treatment
The drug vincristine is derived from the evergreen plant known as the rose periwinkle. Another member of this plant family, the greater periwinkle, is used by herbalists to treat diabetes. During tests to establish its usefulness as a treatment for this condition, chemists reportedly discovered that it was effective in the treatment of tumors. Vincristine was then developed to treat a variety of cancerous conditions including Hodgkin's disease and lymphatic leukemia.

Soothing treatment
Oil from the flower of the calendula, or marigold, plant is used to make a healing antiseptic ointment that can be applied to inflammations and bruises. Herbalists also recommend an infusion made from its petals as an aid to digestion.

Marigold

Source of courage
Traditional herbalism states that borage dispels melancholy and gives courage. But research has shown that the borage seed contains gamma-linolenic acid, which helps to lower blood pressure.

Borage

Traditional Chinese herbal workers

Oriental approach

The Chinese have been using herbal remedies since at least 3000 B.C., and written records show that as far back as 2000 B.C. Chinese herbalists were using the plant *Ephedra sinica* to treat coughs and asthma. Today many cough medicines contain ephedrine, which is found in that plant.

Sweet treatment

The leaves of the flower sweet rocket, or cruciferae, were once used for preventing and curing scurvy. However, a strong dose can also produce vomiting.

Popular cure-all

Ginseng root is the most popular of all traditional Chinese herbal remedies, and is used extensively today to combat fatigue. Prof. E. J. Shellard of London University has supported many of the claims made for ginseng and maintains that "Ginseng has anti-infective and anti-fatigue properties and there is accumulating evidence of its anti-stress activity."

Ginseng

Vital flowers

The leaves of the foxglove plant, or digitalis, have been used for over 200 years in the main drug administered for heart failure. Paradoxically, foxglove is poisonous and should not be consumed.

Healing oil

Herbalists claim that evening primrose oil capsules, made from the seed of the plant, can be used to treat skin conditions and premenstrual tension, along with numerous other ailments such as arthritis, cardiovascular disease, alcoholism, and anorexia nervosa.

Evening primrose

Sweet rocket

Digitalis

When a muscle is "tested," kinesiologists believe it reveals vital information about a patient's state of health.

READING THE BODY

There are a number of diagnostic techniques embraced by New Age healers that examine closely one part of the organism — the muscles or the eye, or the mineral content of the blood, sweat, or hair, for example — in order to analyze the condition of the whole body.

OST HOLISTIC THERAPIES rely to some degree on observing certain aspects of the patient, from skin color and posture to voice tone. Some New Age techniques, however, concentrate on the detailed study of one part or aspect of the body as a means of identifying a wide range of problems that may exist in other areas throughout the body.

Applied kinesiology

By itself, the term "kinesiology" refers to the science of testing muscles to determine their range of movement and muscle tone. Applied kinesiology, developed in 1965 by American chiropractor George Goodheart, develops this concept more fully and uses extensive and painstaking muscle testing to diagnose disease.

When a muscle is "tested," kinesiologists believe, it reveals vital information about a patient's state of health — information that cannot be obtained in any other way. This, its supporters maintain, is because applied kinesiology detects imbalances at an extremely early stage, long before other tests, even X-rays, might reveal ailments that the imbalance might go on to produce. Furthermore, they claim a great deal of information concerning a person's general health and fitness can be generated in seconds.

Weak muscles

According to Dr. Goodheart, many muscles are connected to each other and to specific organs by what he calls energy meridians. Special tests can reveal sluggish or weak muscles. In theory, adherents suggest, the reactivation of such weak muscles can lead to a marked increase of energy flow and a corresponding relief from either general stress or specific symptoms.

To test a muscle, the practitioner raises one of the patient's limbs (chosen according to the muscle being tested), then pushes it steadily downward, instructing the patient to resist. If the resistance is weak, the kinesiologist will apply pressure to the relevant energy points to strengthen the muscle; once this has been accomplished, all muscles will be retested to determine if the body's energy system is balanced.

A course of instruction in these techniques, called Touch for Health, has been developed by a group of American chiropractors to teach lay people the

SOMATOTYPES

"Let me have men about me that are fat....Yon Cassius has a lean and hungry look....Such men are dangerous." So said Shakespeare's Julius Caesar, voicing the ancient belief that personality traits are reflected in an individual's physical shape and bearing. As early as the fifth century B.C., the Greek physician Hippocrates surmised that body shape might be used to diagnose disease. He identified two human classifications: *Habitus phthisicus*, who had long, thin bodies and were prone to respiratory weakness, and *Habitus apoplecticus*, who were short and thickset, and liable to suffer from vascular disease.

The three body types

The best-known modern system of body typing is that of American psychologist W. H. Sheldon. Sheldon's "somatotyping" (from the Greek *soma*, meaning body) involves three "components" of physique that are combined in different degrees in each individual. Endomorphy is the predominance of fat, with a structurally round body shape; mesomorphy indicates the predominance of muscle; and ectomorphy a long, slim body.

Calculating types

In categorizing individuals, each component is given a number from one to seven, with seven representing the highest concentration of that component. Thus, an extreme endomorph would have the somatotype 7-1-1, an extreme mesomorph 1-7-1, and an extreme ectomorph 1-1-7. These pure types are, however, rare. The average human build has a somatotype of about 3-4-4.

Sheldon's original system included links with personality and predisposition to disease, but these are no longer used. The system is now mainly employed as a practical means of describing a particular human physique.

Muscle testing
Elaine Shillitoe, an applied kinesiologist, raises a patient's arm to test the strength of her muscles.

principles of applying the tests and the therapies associated with applied kinesiology. Once trained, they may treat themselves for ailments such as low energy, weight loss or gain, backache, dyslexia, weak eyesight, and stress.

Iridology

It was the ancient Chinese and Japanese who first peered into the human eye to diagnose illness. Later both Chaldean and Egyptian medical theory suggested that eyes held medical significance. Modern iridology, however, is based on the work of a 19th-century physician, Ignatz von Peczely, who believed that the condition of the eyes, and in particular the iris, can reveal past, present, and future disease and weakness in every part of the body.

Born in Hungary in 1822, the young Peczely was a keen ornithologist. One day, treating an owl

The inside story
This diagram, dating from 1504, relates the various parts of the eye to the soul.

with a broken leg, he detected a curious dark line in the bird's eye that disappeared as the leg healed. Later, having qualified as both an engineer and a doctor, Peczely noticed that the human eye seemed to undergo similar changes during illness.

Although Peczely developed a chart of the iris showing different areas relating to various organs and parts of the body, it was a California-based doctor, Bernard

> Ignatz von Peczely believed that the condition of the eyes, and in particular the iris, can reveal past, present, and future disease and weakness in every part of the body.

Jensen, who, during the 1950's, drew up the "maps" of both irises (the right iris corresponding to the right side of the body, and the left iris to the left side) that are used by modern iridologists. Author of the main reference work on the subject, *The Science and Practice of Iridology*, Dr. Jensen divided each iris into sections, like slices of a pie, which are linked to parts or functions of the body, and also into six rings, or zones, associated with bodily systems such as the nervous system and the circulatory system. The practitioner uses the pigmentation and particular markings in these various sections and zones in an attempt to establish a diagnosis or pinpoint weaknesses.

An orthodox view

Medical doctors too note the general appearance of the eyes — whether they are unnaturally bright or yellowish, for example — and examine them and the retina within for signs of specific conditions such as atherosclerosis, diabetes, tuberculosis, and syphilis. Orthodox medicine, however, does not recognize the links between the iris and the parts of the body as detailed on Dr. Jensen's chart.

Although doctors do not consider iridology in itself to be harmful, some fear that relying on this method of diagnosis may prevent people with serious illnesses from seeking the life-saving treatment they need.

Mineral analysis

Naturopaths sometimes measure the levels of major minerals and trace elements in the body by analyzing tissues such as hair, sweat, and blood. Hair and sweat in particular contain not only major minerals like potassium, calcium, and magnesium, and trace elements such as iron, copper, and zinc, but also metals that can be dangerously toxic, such as lead and aluminum.

Although these analyses are relatively straightforward, the way in which they are interpreted is not supported by medical orthodoxy. Doctors doubt that they have any usefulness as diagnostic tools or aids.

PHRENOLOGY

The theory behind the pseudoscience known as phrenology was developed by an Austrian physician, Franz Joseph Gall (1758–1828), who originally called his study "organology," or "cranioscopy." Gall believed the brain consisted of 26 separate organs, each responsible for an emotion such as anger or melancholy, or an innate ability, such as intellectual reasoning, music, or drawing; he even considered religious belief and tendency to criminal behavior to be controlled in the same way. All these organs, or "faculties" as Gall called them, were thought to cause separate swellings on the skull that could be felt from the outside.

A popular science

It was a pupil of Gall's, Johann Kaspar Spurzheim (1776–1832), who dubbed the new study phrenology, adding further faculties to Gall's list, and undertaking a lecture tour in Britain and the United States, where his theories were used unsuccessfully in the treatment of the insane, the rehabilitation of criminals, and the education of children.

At the height of its popularity, phrenology was embraced by every level of society, with Presidents Van Buren, Taylor, and McKinley inviting practitioners to the White House, and Queen Victoria having her children's heads read. By the end of the

Brain size
Phrenology relied on measuring the skull to determine the level of a person's intellect.

century, almost every prosperous home had phrenological charts or busts.

Today we know that certain abilities are situated in different parts of the brain (the left hemisphere generally controls speech and reason, for example, while the right is involved with intuition and spatial ability). The theories of Gall and Spurzheim have been discredited, however, by one simple reality: that the shape of an individual's skull bears little if any relationship to the shape and function of the brain contained within it.

Mapping the brain
This 19th-century ceramic bust is a phrenological guide. It purports to show the sites in the brain of various characteristics.

IRIS ANALYSIS

Sheelagh Colton, director of the Society of British Iridologists, analyzed this patient's eyes, and reported on the color of the iris and the markings on its surface. Her recommendation was that the patient monitor her stress levels and beware of stomach and gynecological problems.

Assessing the constitution

This patient's eyes reportedly reveal that she has a biliary constitution and is prone to liver and gall bladder problems.

WINDOWS OF THE SOUL

Iridologists claim that by examining the various markings on the iris they are able to gain unparalleled insights into the workings of the human body.

MODERN IRIDOLOGY is an alternative diagnostic technique. As such, it is not recognized by medical doctors. The technique can do little harm, however, some doctors feel, so long as it does not delay patients from seeking medical help for serious illnesses. Trained iridologists normally refer patients to traditional medical doctors if they suspect the presence of a disease.

Iridology reportedly aims to reveal weaknesses that may develop into disease as well as pinpointing any illness that the patient has at the time of the examination.

The iridology examination

The iridologist examines the patient's eyes, using various instruments, such as a magnifying glass called a loupe, and a flashlight. Photographs of the iris may also be taken. These photographs then form part of the patient's medical record and can be used to chart the progress of any illness.

In addition to spotting suspected illnesses, iridology, practitioners claim, is also used to pinpoint a patient's inherent strengths and weaknesses. Charts, called iris topographs, relate parts of the body to various areas in the iris. After the examination, the iridologist will usually refer the patient to a specialist for treatment. The specialist might be an alternative therapist, such as a naturopath, or an orthodox doctor, depending on the type of illness indicated.

Signs of illness

Dark flecks such as this reportedly indicate that the patient has a low blood sugar level. Symptoms of this condition are a craving for chocolate, mood swings, sudden fatigue, and light-headedness.

The frill

The area within the frill (the part of the eye closest to the pupil) represents the digestive system, iridologists believe. In this patient, spasm channels (dark, wedge-shaped markings) indicate that too much stress would be likely to lead to stomach problems.

The left eye
This chart, known as an iris topograph, is divided into different sections, reportedly showing which areas on the left side of the body are linked to the iris.

Stress-related illness

A pale ring within the iris is said to be a sign of stress. When stress becomes acute, this patient, iridologists suggest, may experience problems in the weaker areas of her body: the ovaries, uterus, and digestive system.

A stressful color

This eye is hazel in color, which is a mixture of brown and blue. Individuals with this color eye are said by iridologists to have a transitional constitution. They are supposedly more prone to stress than those with pure brown or blue eyes.

A HISTORICAL VIEW

Over 4,000 years ago, the Chinese used the eyes to diagnose various physical ailments. They believed that the eyes mirrored the internal organs, providing a window on the inner workings of the body. The iris was thought to reveal the state of the liver, while the pupil related to the kidneys. The upper eyelid showed the spleen, the lower eyelid the stomach, and the white of the eye the lungs. The inner and outer corners of the eye provided a view of the heart and digestive system.

Three thousand years later, Paracelsus (1493–1541), famed throughout Renaissance Europe as a magician, surgeon, and healer, devised a system of evaluating the health of the body through the appearance of the eye.

It was the Hungarian physician Ignatz von Peczely who developed iridology in its present form during the 19th century. Peczely attempted to establish parallels between areas in the iris and the parts of the body.

Lacunae

Lacunae are gaps in the structure of the iris that indicate where problems may develop. This position, iridologists claim, correlates to the ovary, and indicates a potential for problems there.

A sign of weakness

Corresponding to the weakness in the ovary shown on the other side of the iris, this separation of fibers supposedly indicates a potential weakness in the uterus. Menstrual problems, such as fibroids, may be present or may develop in the future.

The right eye
This iris topograph of the right eye reveals the positions in the eye of the different organs and parts of the body on the right side.

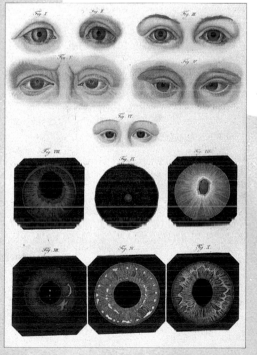

Charting the iris
This illustration, published in Germany in 1838, maps the colors and the markings of the iris.

CHAPTER SIX

HEALING THE PSYCHE

Since Freud devised his revolutionary theories, many of those influenced by him have considered neurosis to be rooted in the experiences of early childhood. To release these experiences, some modern psychotherapies advocate extremes of emotional expression.

"The future will probably attribute far greater importance to psychoanalysis as the science of the unconscious than as a therapeutic procedure." So wrote Sigmund Freud, the founder of psychoanalysis, in 1926. He was remarkably prescient. Even during his lifetime, the technique he had pioneered to identify and treat neurosis was being widely questioned, and even actively challenged by other forms of psychotherapy. But what has rarely been disputed is the significance of Freud's exploration of the unconscious. His

Explorer of the psyche
By investigating the workings of the unconscious, Sigmund Freud (1856–1939) revolutionized our concept of the human psyche and laid the foundations for many forms of psychotherapy.

Classifier of the personality
The Swiss psychologist Carl Gustav Jung (1875–1961) broke away from Freud's theories to found analytic psychology. Among his celebrated concepts is that of extrovert and introvert personality types.

revolutionary theories about the human psyche rank with the theories of Darwin and Einstein in terms of impact on modern Western thought — and Freud's work has created the foundation for the growth and development of various psychotherapies, orthodox and alternative, ever since.

Hysteria and hypnosis
Born in Moravia (now part of Czechoslovakia) in 1856, Freud moved with his family to Vienna when he was three years old and remained there until 1938, the year before his death. He trained as a doctor and in 1886 began practicing as a neurologist. Many of Freud's patients suffered from hysteria (a mental disorder characterized by emotional outbursts), and he treated them using hypnosis, a method pioneered by Jean-Martin Charcot.

Under hypnosis the patient would often recall traumatic episodes from childhood, and this painful process seemed to help effect a cure. In addition, Freud noticed that many of these traumas related to sexual experiences. In 1895 Freud and Josef Breuer, a colleague, published *Studies on Hysteria*. In this they argued that the original trauma produced an emotional energy that was repressed by the conscious mind. Thus blocked, it found expression in neurosis. Recall of the trauma during hypnosis acted as a release, they theorized, and thus the pent-up energy was discharged and the symptoms disappeared.

The birth of psychoanalysis
The limiting factor with hypnosis was that it would not work with every patient. Fortunately, Freud and Breuer discovered a new technique that was just as successful. This became known as free association. The patient relaxed on a couch and was encouraged to talk freely about anything that came into his or her head, however absurd. Gradually, over many sessions of exploring these random

> # The unconscious was not a concept that Freud invented, yet he was the first to explore it in depth and to argue for the awesome reality of its influence in our daily lives.

associations, the analyst hoped to find in the patient's unconscious the keys to the neurosis. Thus psychoanalysis was born.

From 1895 to 1899 Freud analyzed his own dreams in depth, and in 1900 he published his first major psychoanalytic work, *The Interpretation of Dreams*. Freud believed that repressed desires were revealed more often during sleep because the conscious mind was not able to censor them. Because so many repressed desires are sexual, Freud believed that many dream images symbolize sexual organs — for example, a snake or stick might represent the penis, and a box or cupboard the vagina.

In *The Interpretation of Dreams*, Freud set out a major rendering of his theory of the unconscious mind. The unconscious was not a concept that Freud invented, yet he was the first to explore it in depth and to argue for the awesome reality of its influence in our daily lives. In *Psychopathology of Everyday Life* (1901) he suggested that the unconscious was responsible for those verbal errors that have become known as Freudian slips.

Infantile sexuality
Four years later Freud produced another major work: *Three Essays on Sexuality*. In this Freud suggested that

libido (generalized desire for gratification, largely sexual) first appears during infancy. According to Freud, it begins with an oral stage: the infant's first satisfaction is sucking. Then comes the anal stage: retaining and eliminating feces. Then, at the age of about four or five, comes the phallic stage: enjoyment of any genital stimulation.

Freud believed that excessive gratification or frustration of these instincts had important effects on adult behavior. He also put forward the idea of an Oedipus complex. During the phallic stage, the concept suggests, a boy unconsciously desires his mother, sees his father as his rival, feels hostile toward him, and so feels guilty about his sexual feelings and fears castration. The individual's later capacity for mature, healthy, adult relationships, Freud theorized, depended on how well he resolved this early conflict.

Ego and id
Later in his career Freud turned toward describing the development of the psyche. In *The Ego and the Id* (1923) he suggested that the psyche consists of three separate but interacting forces. The most primitive is the id, the source of instinctual energy, the expression of which is experienced as pleasure. Mediating between the id and the outside world is the ego, which takes account of reality, of the past and the future, and is prepared to sacrifice immediate gratification for long-term reward. The superego in turn is concerned with morality and passes judgment on the aims of the id and ego.

During the first decades of the 20th century, Freud helped develop a school of psychoanalysts in Vienna. But conflicts arose, and some colleagues, notably Carl Gustav Jung and Alfred Adler, left to pursue their own theories.

Alternative treatments
Freudian psychoanalysis also came in for considerable criticism. Treatment was regarded as too long and expensive; emphasis on past trauma was seen as unhealthy. The "shrink" (as the psychoanalyst came to be known) became the butt of numerous jokes. As a result, many analysts set out to discover

Investigator of inferiority feelings
The Austrian psychiatrist Alfred Adler (1870–1937), once a close associate of Freud, is famous for his theory about what is now popularly known as the inferiority complex. Adler believed feelings of inadequacy might result from some physical disability or "defect," such as extreme shortness.

shorter, and often less verbal, methods of psychotherapy. Underlying all the new methods, however, was a fundamental acceptance of Freud's emphasis on the importance of the unconscious and of repressed desires and fears. This is eloquent testimony to the power of Freud's ideas and the impact they have had on modern life.

WILHELM REICH
Wilhelm Reich (1897–1957) was an Austrian-born psychoanalyst who broke away from Freud's circle. Far from disowning Freud's emphasis on sexuality as a root cause of psychic troubles, as some of his colleagues had done, Reich took this emphasis even further. In his view — as set out in his book *The Function of the Orgasm* (1927) — complete sexual fulfillment was essential for bodily and mental health.

Muscular locking
Reich also believed that, from an early age, people tense certain muscles as a defense against intolerable feelings. This blocked the flow of energy, he felt, and gave a person his or her characteristic facial expression, manner of speaking, and even body configuration. Certain muscular lockings, he believed, occurred at certain ages.

In treatment Reich made his patients undress and encouraged them to hit out, scream, and cry, so that they might achieve satisfactory sexual expression.

Orgone boxes
Reich identified bodily energy with the cosmic life force, which he termed orgone energy. In the 1940's, after he had settled in the U.S., he decided that orgone energy could be used to treat cancer and other diseases. He claimed to be able to collect and store the energy in the cubicle-like "orgone boxes" he constructed with alternating layers of organic and inorganic materials. A patient would sit in a box for up to half an hour to be "irradiated."

In 1956 federal authorities imprisoned Reich for failing to obey an order to stop selling his orgone boxes, which they regarded as fraudulent. The following year he died of a heart attack.

During the last decade or so of his life Reich was perceived as a crank. After his death, many of his ideas fell into disrepute. Yet during the past 20 years, interest in them has revived and they have helped form the basis of some varieties of New Age psychotherapy, most notably bioenergetics.

Wilhelm Reich

JOURNEYS TO HEALTH

Playacting, returning to the trauma of birth, reliving and expressing childhood distress — these and other forms of modern psychotherapies have much the same basic aim: to enable the individual to reestablish contact with the painful past and obtain release from it.

UCH OF PSYCHOTHERAPY is based on the Freudian principle of encouraging the patient to relive past traumas, traumas that may be buried in the unconscious, and may lie at the very root of the patient's psychological problems. By doing this, various therapies suggest the patient may be able to exorcize the pain and trigger the release of blocked emotional energies. Where individual forms of therapy differ is in the techniques used to enable the patient to reexperience the past and move beyond it.

Gestalt therapy

One active, dramatic, and cathartic form of therapy is known as Gestalt (German for "organized whole" or "shape"), founded by Berlin psychoanalyst Frederick Perls. In one approach to treatment, described in

> # Gestalt therapists encourage the patient to become aware of tensions, hesitations, and other restrictions in speech and body language.

simplest terms, the patient projects one part of the self onto an object (an empty chair, for example) and another part, one that he or she believes is in conflict with the first, onto another object. He or she, with the therapist's help, then begins a dialogue between the two. This serves to bring out the inner conflict.

Gestalt therapists encourage the patient to become aware of tensions, hesitations, and other restrictions in his or her speech and body language. The patient is then shown that this behavior, originally adopted to deal with an event in the past (usually traumatic) is no longer relevant to the present and can be changed.

Gestalt therapy may induce a great release of emotion concerning the past, usually anger or sadness. This is often followed by a reevaluation of present life.

Bioenergetics

Aspects of Gestalt therapy are also found in what is termed bioenergetics, founded by Alexander Lowen, an American follower of Wilhelm Reich. Lowen believed,

HEALING ACT

One technique of making a patient reexperience the painful past to obtain release from it is a form of playacting known as psychodrama. This was developed by Jacob Moreno, a Viennese contemporary of Freud. Moreno's basic idea was that each of us has inside us various selves crying out for expression, and the conflict between them is responsible for anxiety and tension.

Emotional release

In a typical psychodrama session one patient, known as the protagonist, decides on the play, choosing scenes that will dramatize his or her particular problems. The patient plays whichever self he or she wants to dramatize, the therapist acts as director, other patients play various figures in the patient's life, such as friends or members of the family, and the rest form the audience, who are encouraged by the therapist to give active feedback to the protagonist.

In this way the patient is able to explore problems, by bringing them out into the open, and to achieve catharsis (emotional release). Such release may take a dramatic, even explosive, form.

like Reich, that any past emotional trauma causes muscular tension. This gives the body a particular shape. In bioenergetics, the patient exaggerates the tension, then releases it, to enable the memory of the trauma to return. It may then be explored with the therapist.

Appropriate exercise

To put muscles under stress, Lowen and his followers developed exercises— some taken from such diverse sources as skiing and tai chi, an ancient Chinese system of movements. Exercises were selected to relate to the patient's body shape, which was thought to reveal the stage of development at which the trauma occurred.

Lowen had a patient who, as she exercised, had the "absurd" sensation of being beaten by her mother with an iron skillet — absurd because she could not recall that it had ever happened. Yet her mother reportedly admitted that it had. During therapy, as the patient re-enacted the beating, she realized how she still braced herself for the blows. From then on she found that she had more energy and held her body more positively.

Primal scream therapy

Originated in the late 1960's by American psychotherapist Arthur Janov, primal

scream therapy is an attempt to treat neurosis by identifying a primal psychological pain in the patient's life . It has been heavily criticized and rejected by most traditional therapists. "Primal" in Janov's therapy means "fundamental, significant." It refers to a traumatic childhood realization, usually occurring

> **The patient's body shape was thought to reveal the stage of development at which the trauma occurred.**

between the ages of five and seven, that the person is not loved for what he or she is. According to Janov, this leads the child to bury its real self beneath the more acceptable one developed to please its parents. It is this repression of the true self and the resultant denial of true feelings that, Janov believes, is responsible for adult neurosis.

Primal scream therapy is aimed at getting the patient to reexperience primal pain. This may take weeks and may result in the patient sobbing, writhing on the floor, and screaming. It is claimed that reliving the pain expels it, so the patient can begin to experience genuine feelings.

Rebirthing

Invented in 1962 by the Californian alternative health practitioner Leonard Orr, rebirthing is also supposed to take the patient back to childhood, and sometimes to the physical, psychological, and spiritual trauma of birth. Followers of this highly controversial form of therapy claim that reliving this experience enables the patient to be released from birth trauma and so lead a more fulfilled life.

Transactional analysis

Very different from such dramatic forms of self-exploration is what is known as transactional analysis, developed by U.S. psychiatrist Eric Berne. Berne believes the social transactions in any relationship often take the form of unconscious "games." In a marriage, for example, the players may adopt such roles as "If It Weren't For You" and "Look How Hard I've Tried."

Playing such games instead of establishing sincere relationships,

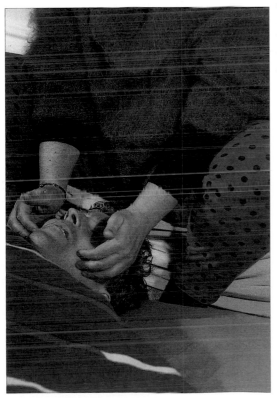

Return to childhood
A therapist helps to guide a patient through the rebirthing experience.

Berne theorizes, can exacerbate psychological problems. By analyzing the games with the patient, the analyst enables him or her to understand the relationship better.

Rogerian therapy

Also known as client-centered therapy or counseling, Rogerian therapy was named after its founder, the well-respected American psychoanalyst Carl Rogers. According to this approach, the client (patient) tells his or her story, and the empathetic consultant (therapist) nods or repeats back key words. This encourages the client to delve more deeply into the problem, often with the release of powerful blocked emotions.

Some of these alternative forms of psychotherapy may be more effective than others; some may do no good at all. Yet most are indeed derived from Freud's theories, and in some cases, and in certain circumstances, may provide some benefit. It must be stressed, therefore, that such therapies should never be regarded as replacements for more conventional forms of psychotherapy and psychoanalysis; these proven, professional approaches should always be a patient's first resort.

Images of pain
Ever since Carl Gustav Jung introduced art therapy as part of his treatment of neurosis, it has been a valued psychotherapeutic technique. By means of painting, the patient expresses his or her inner turmoil and perhaps provides clues to the repressed secret in the past that lies at the root of the pain.

Back to School

"I was on my knees, still punching the pillow and yelling....Then I collapsed in tears, feeling again just how alone I had felt at school."

JOHN R., A UNIVERSITY LECTURER, had just finished seeing a psychoanalyst. The treatment had eased his problems, but he sensed that it had encouraged his tendency to think rather than to feel. He decided to enroll in a weekend workshop in bioenergetics, a therapy in which physical expression is used to release the emotions. He tells here what happened.

"The two group leaders, Alan and Jane, got us to do preliminary exercises. During these we tensed and relaxed our muscles, and concentrated on breathing. "We then worked in pairs. Jane asked us to make fists and call 'No' or 'Don't' to our partner. Bob, my partner, and I just went through the motions. Alan put a pillow between us and told us to try to be more aggressive. I started punching the pillow harder and shouting, 'Don't....'

"'Don't! Don't! Don't!' Suddenly my mind was full of the pain I'd felt when my parents had sent me away to school. Then Bob started to look like the school bully. Suddenly Alan was at my side. He was my father and I was saying, 'Why don't you believe me?' By this time I was on my knees, still punching the pillow and yelling.

Jane became my mother

"Jane became my mother. I shouted at her, 'Why don't you believe me either?' Then I collapsed in tears, feeling again just how alone I had felt at school. Afterward Jane told me to breathe deeply.

"Then some of the group gently massaged me. Alan told us how academic people often seek refuge in the mind from hurts and abandonment. Jane explained why none of this had emerged during my psychoanalysis: 'This is bioenergetics. The mind forgets traumas, but the body always remembers.' The group broke up. Suddenly I felt happy and very much alive."

Publisher's note: Bioenergetics is a controversial therapy that cannot be recommended as a substitute for conventional psychoanalysis or psychotherapy.

CASEBOOK
MOTHER LOVE

"The pain began to dissipate. I continued my rhythmic breathing....I had the sensation of feeling secure in familiar surroundings."

SUSAN D., A BOOK EDITOR, hoped that being rebirthed would improve communication in her relationships. She went to see Anne, who had been rebirthing people for 15 years in Los Angeles and London. Susan tells us what happened.

"The rebirthing room at Anne's apartment was warm and softly lit and was furnished with comfortable armchairs. A mattress, pillows, and blankets were in one corner of the room. I sat on the mattress, feeling like a child sitting up in bed about to be read a bedtime story. When I felt ready to start I lay down and covered myself with blankets until I felt completely warm and comfortable.

Rhythmic breathing
"Anne explained how by setting up a continuous rhythm of inhaling and exhaling, I could get in touch with my inner feelings. I placed one hand on my belly and the other hand on my chest, and kept my jaw relaxed and my mouth open. I began to breathe deeply and rhythmically. Anne stayed at my side the whole time, encouraging me.
"For about 15 minutes I maintained this rhythmic inhaling and exhaling.

Suddenly I began to experience a severe pain deep in my lower abdomen. I was in pain every time I breathed. Very gently Anne talked me through it: the rhythmic breathing had brought some emotional blockage into consciousness. The pain was distracting me from looking at what it represented.

Quiet, warm, and dark
"Anne encouraged me to continue the deep rhythm of my breathing, bringing my breath right down into the area that was causing pain. When the pain still persisted she suggested that I try panting so that I breathed only from the chest for a while.
"I did not want to give in to the distraction of the pain. Soon the pain began to dissipate. I continued my rhythmic breathing. It was no longer an effort. I had the sensation of feeling secure in familiar surroundings. There were familiar smells. Where had I experienced this before? Then I had a childhood memory: at a theater I had been sitting next to my mother, and in that quiet, warm, and dark moment when the lights go down before the play begins I had been overwhelmed by the sensation of nuzzling up to her. I was re-experiencing that same feeling.

A strong bond
"Whatever conflicts or difficulties there may be in my relationship with my mother, I was now able to acknowledge the strength of the bond between us.
"When I opened my eyes I felt as relaxed as if I had slept for a week. That night I slept like a baby."

Publisher's note: Rebirthing is a controversial therapy that cannot be recommended as a substitute for conventional psychoanalysis or psychotherapy.

INDEX

Page numbers in **bold** type refer to illustrations and captions.

A

Aborigines, 53, 88, 100
Abrams, Albert, 99
Absent healing, 53
Acupressure, 20, 115, **116**
Acupuncture, 20, **20**, 66, 68, 70-71, **70, 71**
Addictions, 48, 70
Adelaide, Queen, 43
Ader, Robert, 48
Adler, Alfred, 135, **135**
Affirmation, 92-94, 97
Agate, **90**
Aging, 28
Agpaoa, Antonio ("Doctor Tony"), **65**
AIDS, 49
Akuaba figures, **36**
Albert, Prince, **43**, 129
Alcoholism, 125
Alcott, Louisa May, 42
Alexander, Albert, 109
Alexander, F.M., 108, 109, **109**
Allergies, 121, **121**
Alpha Stim machine, 95
Alternative Therapy (report), 102
Amanita muscaria (mushroom), 33
American Indians, 14, **33**, 56, 88, 100
Amethyst, **90**
Amulets, 36, **36**, **37**, 86, 88, **88**
Analytic Psychology, **134**
Anand, Bal Krishnan, 75
Anderson, Mary, 84
Andrews, Dr. Edson, 85
Animals, 27, 33, 39, 71, **71**, 76
Annett, Stephen, 73
Anorexia nervosa, 125
Anthroposophical Society, 23, **23**
Antimony, 24
Antoni, Dr. Michael, 49
Apothecaries, **20**, **35**
Aristotle, 32
Aromatherapy, 22, 84
Arsenic (*Arsenicum album*), 39
Artemisia moxa, 68, 70
Arteriotomy (venesection), 24, 26
Arthritis, 27, 28, 77, 121, 125
Art therapy, **139**
Asclepius, 30, **32**, **37**
Aspasia, 32
Assessing the Safety and Efficacy of Medical Technology (report), 27
Asthma, 40, 47, 48, 77, 108, **125**
Astrology, 85
Atalanta (G. Hargreaves), **86**
Atherosclerosis, 129
Atlantis, 86-88, **86**
Auras, 22, 90-91, 100-101
photography, 104-105, **104, 105**
Australia, 53, 88, 100, 115
Autism, 117
Autobiography of a Yogi (Swami Paramhansa Yogananda), 75, 79
Autosuggestion, 97
Avogadro, Amedeo, 40
Ayurveda, 20, **20**, 76, **76**

B

Bach, Dr. Edward, 84
Bacillary dysentery, 71
Back pain, 27, 77, 128

Badeley, Dr. John, 53
Bagnell, Oscar, 100
Bala, Giri (Fasting saint), 75
Beatles, The, 79, **79**
Beerbohm Tree, Herbert, 109
Beijing, China, **72**
Belgium, shrines, 52
Belladonna (*Aconitum napellus*), 38
Bend, Cynthia, 14
Benjamin, Harold H., **49**
Benson, Dr. Herbert, 49, 92
Berne, Eric, 139
Beyond Feedback (E. and A. Green), 47
Bible, The, 51, **51**, 55, 56
Bioenergetics, 135, 136, 138, 140
Biofeedback, 47, **47**
Birth of a Modern Shaman (C. Bend and T. Wiger), 14, 16
Blackie, Dr. Marjorie, 42
Blackwell, Elizabeth, 35
Blindness, 9-10, 13-14, 16
Blood dialysis, 27
Bloodletting, 24, **24**, 26, **26**
Blood pressure, 118, **124**
Blood sugar, 130
Boddie, Caroline, 90
Book of Sacred Stones, The (B.G. Walker), 89
Borage, **124**
Bouton, Jim, 42
Boyle, Robert, **52**, 86
Braid, James, 48
Brain, **56**, 94, 95, **95**
size, **129**
Brand, Dr. Richard, 21
Brazil, 62, **64**
Breathing exercises, 22, 81
Breuer, Josef, 134
Brezhnev, Leonid, 54
Britain, 63, 77, 115
British Columbia, Canada, 33, 37
British Honduras, 88
Bronchitis, 76, 77
Brown, R., 81
Buddhism, 96, **96**
Buling, Hans, **29**
Bulloch, Karen, 48
Burkitt, Dr. Denis, 123
Burns, 48

C

Caduceus, **37**
Campbell, Joseph, 35
Canada, 115
Cancer, 27, 28, 49, 58, 59, 97, 123, **124**
diet, 118, 122-123, **123**
stress, 21, 48, 73, 93-94
Capra, Fritjof, 22
Cardiovascular disease, 125
Carnelian, **91**
Carrier Indians, 33
Case for Astrology, The (J. West and J. Toonder), 85
Cassileth, Dr. Barrie, 94
Cayce, Edgar, 61-62, **61**, 86-87
Cerebral palsy, 117
Ceres, 32
Chakras, 80-81, **80**, **81**
Chapman, George, 62
Charcot, Jean-Martin, 48, **48**
Charokh puja (Muslim spring festival), 57
Charms, 36, **36**, **37**
Cheese, 122, **122**
Chemical Abstract Service, 121
Chemicals, allergies, 121
Chi, 53, 66, 68, **68**, 70, 82
shiatsu, 20, 115-116, **116**
Childbirth, 32, 34, **34**, 35

China
acupuncture, 68, 70, **71**
herbalism, 124, **124**, 125, **125**
iridology, 128, 131
life force. *See Chi.*
tai chi, 72-73, **72, 73**
Chiropractic, 20, 22, 114-15, **114, 115**
Cholera epidemic, London 1854, 40, **40**
Chopin, Frédéric, 42
Christian Science, 55
Cinchona (Peruvian bark), 38
Citrine, **91**
Clairvoyance, 101
Clavel, Dr. Carlos, 46
Clement, Pope, 86
Cleopatra, 30
Clover, four-leaf, **36**
Color and Personality (A. Kargere), 84
Color therapy, 81, 84, **84**
Color Therapy (M. Anderson), 84
Colton, Sheelagh, 130
"Company of Undertakers, The" (W. Hogarth), 29
Complete healing systems, 20
Constantino, Fidencio, **54**
Coronary heart disease, 71, 77, 118
Cosmic duality, **111**
Coué Emile, 97, **97**
Coughs, 125
"Country Fair" (T. Rowlandson), **28**
Cranial osteopathy, 117
Crystal
artifacts, 88, **88**, 89, **89**
healing, 86, 88, 89, 90-91, **90, 91**
Cullen, William, 38
Cupping, 26

D

Da Silva, Edivaldo, **64**
Davis, Adele, 120
De Freitas, José, 62-63, **62**
De la Warr, George, 99
Depression, 49, 91
Diabetes, 48, 77, 118, 122, 129
herbalism, **124**
Diagnosis, 22, 98-103, 104-105, 127-131
shiatsu, 116
Dickens, Charles, 42
Diets, 22, 76, 107, 111, 118-120, 122
cancer, 118, 122, 123, **123**
Oriental, 69
vegetarian, 120, **120**
Digestive problems, 121, 122, **124**
Digitalis (foxglove), **125**
Doornik, Belgium, **57**
Drown, Ruth, 99
Drugs, 20, 24, 27, 38, 48
homeopathic, 38-39
Dying, 100-101
Dyslexia, 128

E

Eddy, Mary Baker, 55, **55**
Edwards, Harry, 63, **63**
Ego and the Id, The (S. Freud), 135
Egypt, 30, 78, 88, **88**, 128
Einstein, Albert, 82
Electrical treatment, **27**
Electroencephalograph (EEG), 47, **47**, 94
Elements of the Chakras, The (N. Ozaniec), 81
Elizalde, David and Helen, **65**
Ellison, Prof. Arthur, 103

Emotions, 21, 69, 85, 107, 110, 136
Energy fields, 84, 111
chakras, 80-81, **80, 81**
chi, 53, 68, **68**, 82, 116
England, 26, 32, 34
Ephedra sinica, 125
Epilepsy, 24, 47, 117
Escudero, Dr. Angel, 44, 46, **46**
Esdaile, James, 46
Ethnobotany, 33
Europe, 32, 34, 115
Evening primrose, **125**
Exercises, 107, 108
Extrasensory perception (ESP), 10, 16
Eyes, 24, 128

F

Faith healing, 51, **51**, 52-55, **54**, 58-59
Fakirs, **57**
Fasting, 111
Fatigue, 121, 122, **122**, **125**, 128
Feldenkrais, Moshe, 108, **108**
Felicie, Jacoba, 32
Fire walking, 56, **56**
Fitzgerald, Dr. William, 78
Flagellation, **57**
Flexner report, 41
Flotation tanks, 96
Flower remedies, 84, 124, **124**, **125**
Foot massage, 22, **22**, 78, **78**
France, 51, 52, 97
Frauds, 64, **64-65.**
See also Quacks.
Free association, 134
Freud, Sigmund, 132, 134-135, **134**
Fringe Medicine (B. Inglis), 103
Fritz, Dr. Adolf, 62
Fruit, 118, 119, 120, 122, **122**
Fuller, John G., 62
Function of the Orgasm, The (W. Reich), 135

G

Galen, 27
Gale, Thomas, 34
Gallbladder, 130
Gall, Franz Joseph, 129
Gandhi, Mahatma, **43**
Garlic, 120, **120**, 122
Gattefosse, René-Maurice, 84
"Gentle Emetic, A," **25**
Gestalt therapy, 136
Getting Well Again (Dr. O.C. Simonton), 94
Ginseng, **122**, **125**
Gods, 30-32
Goodheart, George, 127
Gorges, Denis, 95
Graham Potentializer, 95
Gram, Hans, 41
Greatrakes, Valentine, **52**
Greece, 24, 26, 30, 32
Green, Elmer and Alyce, 47
Green goddess, 33, 35
Gunn, Paul, 58
Gynecology, 26-27, 130, 131

H

Hahnemann, Samuel C., 38, **38**, 40, 41
Hair analysis, 22, 129
Hall, Howard R., 48

Hands, laying on, 9, 10, 13-14, 16, 51, 53-54, **104**
Haraldsson, Erlendur, 79
Hargreaves, Gerald, **86**
Harrison, George, **79**
Harvey, William, 26
Hawthorne, Nathaniel, 42
Hay diet (Fundamental eating), 122
Hayfever, 41
Hay, Louise L., 93-94
Hay, William Howard, 122
Headaches, 24, 47, 48, 108, 117, 121
Headbands, crystal, 88
Healing: A Doctor in Search of a Miracle (Dr. W.A. Nolen), 59, 63
Healing mask, **52**
Health via Food (W.H. Hay), 122
Heal Your Body (L.L. Hay), 93
Heart problems, 21, 47, 48, 73, 77, 125
Helen of Troy, 32
Heller, Joseph, 110
Hemi-Sync machine, 95
Herbalism, 20, **20**, 27, 124-125, **124**, 125
    homeopathy, 38, 39
    women, 30, 35
Heterosuggestion. *See* Hypnosis.
Hinduism, **57**, 75, 76, 84, **94**
Hippocrates, 27, 53, 111, 128
Hogarth, William, **29**
Holistic Approach to Cancer, The (Dr. C.B. Pearce), 21
Holistic medicine, 20, 22, 107, 111
Holmes, Oliver Wendell, 24
Homeopathy, 20, 38-42, **41**
Homer (The Odyssey), 32
Horseshoes, **37**
House of Sensory Perception, Denmark, **84**
Humors, 27
Huxley, Aldous, 109
Hyderabad, India, **20**
Hydrotherapy, 22, 26, **26**
Hygeia, 30, 32, **32**
Hypnosis, 46, 48, 97, 134
Hypochondria, **29**
Hysterectomy, 26-27

I

I Believe in Miracles (K. Kuhlman), 58
Immune system, 21, 48-49
Immunization, 41
India, 43, 46, 56, 76
Infectious diseases, 71
Ingham, Eunice D., 78, **78**
Inglis, Brian, 103
Interpretation of Dreams, The (S. Freud), 134
Intuitive diagnosis, 102-103
Ireland, shrines, 52
Iridology, 22, 128-129, **128**, 130, **130, 131**
Iris analysis, 130, **130, 131**
Irving, Sir Henry, 109
Italy, 26, 32, **32**, 51

J

Janov, Arthur, 138
Japan, 115, 128
Jenner, Edward, 41
Jenness, Diamond, 33
Jensen, Dr. Bernard, 128-129
Jesus, 51, **51**
Jewish breastplate, **88**
Joan of Arc's well, Domrémy-la-Pucelle, France, **30**

Jode, Gerard de, **27**
Jolo Serpent Handlers, **57**
Jung, Carl Gustav, **134**, 135

K

Kamiya, Dr. Joe, 46
Kargere, Audrey, 84
Ketchum, Dr. Wesley, 61
Kilner, Walter J., 100
Kinesiology, 22, 127-128, **128**
Kirlian photography, 102-103, **102, 103**
Kirlian, Semyon Davidovich and Valentina, 102-103
Kirsch, Dr. Daniel, 95
Klopfer, Bruno, 49
Kneipp, Sebastian, 26
Kolar, Dr. Francis J., 84
Krieger, Dolores, 54, 102, **103**
Kuhlman, Kathryn, 58-59

L

Ladokh, India, **68**
Laidlaw, Robert W., **62**
Lang, Dr. William, **62**
Langtry, Lily, 109
Larbig, Dr. Wolfgang, **57**
Laroon, M., **29**
Layne, Al, 61
Leeching, **24**, 26
Lennon, John, **79**
Le Shan, Lawrence, 96
Let's Eat Right to Keep Fit (A. Davis), 120
Lex, Dr. Ary, 62
Liébeault, Dr. A.A., 97
Lightning Bird (L. Watson), 33
Lillard, Harvey, 114-115
Little, Sally, 42
Liver, 111, 130
Locke, Dr. Steven, 49
London Homeopathic Hospital, 40, **42**
London Medical Battery Company, **27**
Longfellow, Henry W., 42
Louis, Dr., 26
Lourdes, France, 52, 53
Love, Medicine and Miracles (Dr. B.S. Siegel), 49
Lowen, Alexander, 136, 138
Lu-ch'an, Yang, 72
Lymphocytes, 48, **48**

M

Macrobiotics, 118
Magnetism, 27, 55, 101
Maharishi Mahesh Yogi, 79, **79**, 96
Malleus Maleficarum, 35
Mandalas, **94**
Mandrake, **35**
Many Ways of Being, The (S. Annett), 73
Mapp, Crazy Sally, **29**
Marigold (Calendula), **124**
Massage, 22, **22, 76**, 107, 110, 114, 115
Massage chair, **95**
Mastingly, Mrs. (faith-healing subject), 53
Materia medica, 38, 39
McKinley, President William, 129
Meditation, 22, 77, 96, **96**
    dynamic, 79, 94, 96
    transcendental (TM), 79, 96

Megalithic sites, 88
Menuhin, Sir Yehudi, 42, **43**
Meridians, 68, **68**, 70, **70**, 116
Mesmer, Franz Anton, 55
Metallic tractors, 88
Mexico, crystal skull, 88, **89**
Michael (acupuncture subject), 66, 68, 70
Midwives, 32, 34, **34**, 35
Migraine, 47, 48, 77, 108, 117
Mind, 21, 46, 48-49, 73
    holistic medicine, 39, 107, 108, 110
Mind-programming, 44, 46-47, **47**
Minerals, 27, 39, 124, 129
Miracles Are My Visiting Cards (E. Haraldsson), 79
Mitchell-Hedges, F.A., 89
Monroe, Robert, 95
Moon, 85
Moreno, Jacob, 138, **138**
Moss, Thelma, 103
Motoyama, Dr. H., 81
Moxibustion, 68, **68**, 70
Muladhara, 80, **81**
Muscles, 127-128, **128**
Musculo-skeletal complaints, 110, 112, 114-117
Myanmar, Union of, **96, 116**
Myers, F.W., 53-54
Myss, Caroline, 98

N

Namikoshi, Takujiro, 116
Nature, 33, 35
Naturopathy, 111, 129
Nausea, 115
Nepal, mandalas, **94**
Nervous diseases, 47, 91
New Age movement, 82, 84, 98-99, 127-128
    crystal therapy, 80, 90
    relaxation, 92-94, 96
New Guinea, 88
New Zealand, 115
Nicol, Dr. John, 71
Noesitherapy, 46, **46**
Nolen, Dr. William A., 59, 63
Northcote, James, **34**
Nuns, 34, **34**

O

Occidental Mythology: The Masks of God (J. Campbell), 35
Occult Medicine Can Save Your Life (Dr. C. Norman Shealy), 103
O'Connor, Barbara, 53
Octavia, 32
Oedipus complex, 135
Olivier, Sir Laurence, 42
Orr, Leonard, 139
Osteoarthritis, 77
Osteopathy, 20, 112, **112**, 114, **114**
    cranial, 115
Ousley, S.G.J., 101
Outline of Spiritual Healing, The (G. Turner), 100
Ozaniec, Naomi, 81

P

Pain relief, 35, 48, 78, 84
    acupuncture, 68, 70, 71
Pakistan, 76

Palmer, Daniel David, 114-115
Paracelsus, 20, 131
Paraguay, **64**
Pasteur, Louis, 63, **63**
Patanjali (*Yoga Sutra*), 75
Pattern of Health, The (Dr. A. Westlake), 103
Payadore, Dr. F., 46
Pearce, Dr. I.C.B., 21
Peczely, Ignatz von, 128, 131
Pendulums, 98, **102**
Penny, 70
Periwinkle, rose, **124**
Perkins, Dr. Elisha, 88
Perls, Frederick, 136
Personality, 21, 39, 101, 108, **134, 135**
    diets, 69, 76
    humors, 27, **27**
Peyote cactus, 33
Philippines, 64, **65**
Photographs, electromagnetic, 104-105, **104, 105**
Phrenology, 129, **129**
Placebos, 46, 89
Plants, 84, **105**.
    See also Herbalism.
Plato, 86
Pliny the Elder, 32
Polarity therapy, 111
Pollution, chemicals, 121
Portugal, shrines, 52
Posture, 20, 21, 108, 109
Power rods, 88
Prana, 53
Preissnitz, Vincenz, 26
Premenstrual tension, 125
Primal scream therapy, 138
Psychic healers, 61-63, 64, **64, 65**
Psychoanalysis, 107, 132, 134
Psychodrama, 138, **138**
Psychoneuroimmunology (PNI), 48
Psychopathology of Everyday Life (S.Freud), 134
Psychosomatic illnesses, 21, 48-49
Psychotherapies, 132, 134-135, 136, 138-139
Puharich, Dr. Andrija, 62
Purging, 24
Pythias (wife of Aristotle), 32

Q

Quacks, 28-29, **28, 29**
Quartz, 86, 88-89, **89**, 90-91, **90, 91**
Quevedo, Father, **64**
Quimby, Phineas, 55
Quin, Frederick Foster, 40
Qusta ibn-Luqa, 89

R

Radiesthesia, 98-99, **102**
Radionics machine, 99, 102, 103
Ragland, Dr. David, 21
Rajneesh, Bhagwan Shree, 79
Ramakrishna, Sri Paramhansa, 79
Ramirez, Dr. Amanda, 48
Randi, James, **65**
Ravitz, Dr. Leonard, 85
Rawlins, Michael, 27
Read, William, **28**
Rebirthing, 139, **139**, 141
Reflexology, 21, 22, **22**, 78, **78**
Reich, Wilhelm, 135, **135**
Relaxation, 22, 72-73, 77, 92-93, 94, 110
    biofeedback, 47, **47**
Relics, holy, 51

Remen, Dr. Rachel Naomi, 35
Report on Radionics (E. Russell),
  99, 102
Rheumatism, 35, 77
Riley, Pat, 42
Rockefeller, John D., Sr., **42**
Rogers, Carl, 139
Rolf, Dr. Ida, 110, **110**
Roman Catholic Church, 51, 53
Rome, 26, 32, **32**
Romeo Error, The (L. Watson), 64
Rossner, Marilyn, 10, 13-14
Rowlandson, Thomas, **28**
Rrasebe (shamaness), 33
Rush, Benjamin, 26
Russell, Edward, 99, 102

S _____

Sai Baba, Sri Satya, 79
St. Winefride's Well, Holywell,
  Wales, **50**
Sales, Antonio Oliviera, **64**
Salmon, William, 86
Sassafras (Ague tree), **124**
Scarab amulet, **88**
Scarification, 26
Schauss, Alexander, 122
Schizophrenia, 27
Schmidt, Kate, 42
Schwartz, Gary E., 47
*Science and Health with Key to the
  Scriptures* (M.B. Eddy), 55
Science and Practice of Iridology
  (Dr. B. Jensen), 129
*Science and the Evolution of
  Consciousness: Chakras, Ki
  and Psi* (Dr. H. Motoyama and
  R. Brown), 81
Scurvy, 125
Self-defense, 73
Self-help, 22, 97
Self-mutilation, **57**
Self-Realization Fellowship, 79
Septem Planetae (G. de Jode), **27**
Serenity, 92-94, 95, 96
Shacter, Dr. Michael, 103
Shamanism, 14, 33, **33**, **37**
Shaw, Eva, 85
Shaw, George Bernard, 109
Shealy, Dr. C. Norman, 103
Sheinkin, Dr. David, 103

Sheldon, W. H., 128
Shellard, Prof. E.J., 124
Shen Nung, Emperor of China, 124
Shiatsu, 20, 115-116, **116**
Shillitoe, Elaine, **128**
Shrines, Holy, 51
Siddhas, 77
Siegel, Dr. Bernie S., 49
Simonton, O. Carl, 94
Simpson, O.J., 42
Simpson, Dr. William Franklin, 55
Sivananda, Swami, 13
Skin irritations, 121
Skull, 89, **89**, 117, **117**
Sleeping Prophet, The (J. Stearn), 61
Smallpox, 41
Smith, Michael, 88-89
Snakes, **37**, 56, **57**
Somatotypes, 128
Soubirous, Bernadette, 52
Spices, **20**
Spine, 108, **109**, 110, 114-115, **114**,
  115, **116**
Spiritual Frontiers Fellowship, 16
Spiritual healing, 22, 63, **64**
Spurzheim, Johann Kaspar, 129
Sri Ramanand Yogi, 75, **75**
Stearn, Jess, 61
Steiner, Rudolf, 23, **23**
Still, Andrew Taylor, 112, 114
Stone, Dr. Randolph, 111
Stress, 21, **21**, 73, 92, 108, 128, 130,
  131
Stress-related illnesses, 21, 47, 48,
  110, 117
Succussion (shaking), 40, **40**
Sun signs, 85
Sutherland, William Garner, 117
Svadhishthana, 80, **80**, 81
Swastika, **36**
Sweet rocket, **125**
Sydenham, Thomas, 26
Syphilis, 129

T _____

Tai chi, 72-73, **72**, **73**, 107
Talbot, Nathan A., 55
Tansley, David, **102**
Tao of Physics, The (F. Capra), 22
Taylor, President Zachary, 129
Teck, duchess of, **42**

Telesphoros, **32**
Thaipusam festival, Singapore, **57**
Therapeutic Touch, The (D. Krieger),
  102-103
Therapeutic Touch (TT), 54, 102-103,
  103
Thirty Years a Spiritual Healer
  (H. Edwards), 63
Thomas, Christina, 56
Three Essays on Sexuality (S. Freud),
  134-135
Tlingit tribe devices, **33**
Toonder, Jan, 85
Touch for Health, 127-128
Trager, Dr. Milton, 108, 110, **110**
Transactional analysis, 139
Transcendental meditation (TM),
  79, 96
Trilha, Ivan, **64**
Trotula, 32, **32**, 34
Tsimshian tribe, **37**
Tuberculosis, 48, 129
Turmeric, 76
Turner, Gordon, 100
Turner, Tina, 42, **42**
Tutankhamen necklace, **37**
"Twain, Mark" (J.M. Flagg), **43**

U _____

Ulcers, 48
U.S.A., 35, 41, 56, **57**, 115, 121
Use of Self, The (F.M. Alexander), 109

V _____

Vaccination, 41
Van Buren, President Martin, 129
Vasectomy, 27
Vedas, 75
Vegetables, 118, 119, 120
Vertebrae, **114**, **115**, **116**
Victoria May, princess of Teck, **42**
Victoria, Queen, **43**, 129
"Village Doctress, The" (J.
  Northcote), **34**
Vincristine, **124**
Vishuddha, 80, **81**
Visualization, 94

Vitamin A, 122, 123
Vivekananda, Swami, 79, **79**
Von Hohenlohe, Father, 53, **53**
Von Reichenbach, Karl Baron, 86

W _____

Wagner, Lindsay, 42
Wakeman, R. John, 48
Walker, Barbara G., 89
Washington, President George, 26
Water, 27, 30, **30**, **40**, **50**, **54**.
  See also Hydrotherapy.
Watson, Lyall, 33, 64
Weir, Sir John, **42**
Wellness Community, Santa Monica,
  California, 49, **49**
Wells, **30**, **50**
West, Dr. D.J., 53
West, John, 85
West, Dr. Philip, 49
Westlake, Dr. Aubrey, 103
Wiger, Tayja, 9-10, 13-14, 16
Wise, Anna, 94
Witches, 34, 35
Wolf spider (*Lycosa tarentula*), **41**
World Health (magazine), 71

Y _____

Yeats, W.B., 42
Yin and Yang, 66, 69, **69**, 70, 118
Yoga, 22, **22**, 53, 74-75, 77, **77**, 79, 107.
  See also Chakras.
Yogananda, Swami Paramhansa,
  75, 79
Yoga Sutra (Patañjali), 75, 77
Your Astrological Guide to Fitness
  (E. Shaw), 85

Z _____

Zambia, **20**
Zen Buddhism, 96, **96**
Zimbabwe, 63
Zodiac, 85, **85**

PHOTOGRAPHIC SOURCES ——